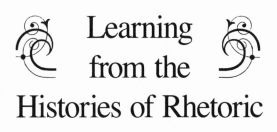

Learning from the Histories of Rhetoric

▼

Essays in Honor of
Winifred Bryan Horner

Edited by Theresa Enos

Southern Illinois University Press
Carbondale and Edwardsville

Library of Congress Cataloging-in-Publication Data

Learning from the histories of rhetoric : essays in honor of Winifred Bryan
Horner / edited by Theresa Enos.
    p.   cm.
   Includes bibliographical references (p.   ) and index.
   1. Rhetoric—History. 2. Rhetoric—Study and teaching. I. Horner,
Winifred Bryan. II. Enos, Theresa.
  P301.L345 1993
  808'.009—dc20   92-19715
  ISBN 0-8093-1784-2 (cloth)   CIP
  ISBN 0-8093-1800-8 (paper)

Frontispiece: Winifred Bryan Horner (Photograph by Carole Patterson)

Contents

Preface

This festschrift for Winifred Bryan Horner offers rhetoric and composition teachers varied perspectives not only on studying our rhetorics of history but also using them. Setting the context for each of the essays that follow, Richard Lloyd-Jones in part 1 interweaves personal and professional history as a pedagogue who uses the history of rhetoric. Thomas P. Miller makes a strong argument for broadening our knowledge of rhetorical traditions and deepening our perceptions of what they can mean to teaching. Donald C. Stewart suggests how we might reach into our history to find a philosophical model for present-day college rhetoric and composition programs. And Edward P.J. Corbett charts the history closest to teachers and administrators in writing programs.

The essays in part 2 specifically show how we can connect past traditions of rhetoric to current pedagogy. Susan C. Jarratt concentrates on Sappho to help us and our students to learn that women's ways of thinking and writing can differ from men's. Marjorie Curry Woods foregrounds writing pedagogy from medieval times, writing techniques that add to our classroom strategies. Both Jean Dietz Moss and Kathleen E. Welch focus on dialectic, Moss showing us how closely dialectic and rhetoric worked together in the Renaissance and Welch continuing the argument for including dialectic in college writing courses. Richard Leo Enos and S. Michael Halloran create strong relationships between classical rhetoric and two present-day approaches to writing: peer collaboration and declamation.

Thus the two parts of this book illuminate that knowing our histories of rhetoric should go beyond the obvious value of studying history for its own sake. For us, studying the rhetorics of history can and should have strong and immediate connections to where we spend much of our time—in the classroom helping students become aware of their many rhetorical choices in various kinds of discourse.

I owe much to Jix Lloyd-Jones and the late Don Stewart who kept me on course as I struggled to visualize a book that would both help teachers use rhetorical traditions and honor Win, who has always connected the study of history to teaching and learning. I thank Tom Miller for insightful suggestions on the arrangement and on my chapter in this festschrift. Deep gratitude goes to Kenney Withers, an editor of vision who has been instrumental in shaping our field of study by publishing important work that doesn't fit the narrow definition of "traditional scholarship." I express sincere appreciation to Carol A. Burns, project editor, and to Sally Master, manuscript editor, who provided valuable assistance throughout the process. Finally, I thank my son Brennan, who is both a writing teacher and an historian and who kept asking me hard questions about practical connections between history and praxis. Attempts to answer those questions led to this collection of essays in honor of Win Horner, whose work in rhetoric is an example of how we might use, and learn from, the histories of rhetoric.

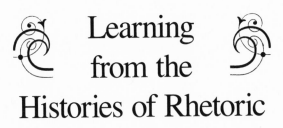

Learning from the Histories of Rhetoric

▼

1

"A Brand New World"
Using Our Professional and
Personal Histories of Rhetoric

Theresa Enos

When Winifred Bryan Horner began her doctoral work at Michigan in 1973, there were only a handful of rhetoric and composition programs in the country, and the history of rhetoric did not have a scholarly base in English departments. What interested her then and now is the place of writing in the humanities, the ways in which human beings think through their ideas and communicate those ideas to others both in written and spoken language. Both her work on writing and literature and her scholarship on history address this core concern.

The area that has proven most fruitful for Win Horner's work has been the history of rhetoric. That for hundreds of years rhetoric, the oldest of the humanities, was the center and ultimate goal of all education furthered Win's particular interest in multidisciplinary writing programs across the country. All of Win's work in the history of rhetoric has stemmed from her view of writing as central to thinking and learning—the cornerstone of education. Her focus on education and her emphasis on teaching/learning connections have helped those of us who do historical scholarship recognize the positive aspects of our need to connect history to teaching.

Coming out of her attempt to create for herself some research synthesis of a field that spans twenty-five centuries and to make strong teaching/learning connections is the most-used bibliography in the history of rhetoric: *The Present State of Scholarship in Historical and Contemporary Rhetoric* (University of Missouri Press, 1983). In 1990 appeared the revised edition of this text that not only has defined the history of rhetoric for twentieth-century scholars but also has become one

3

of our strongest teaching tools because it has taught us how much we have to build on. Besides editing both editions, Win contributed the eighteenth-century bibliographic essay synthesizing the rich Scottish contribution to rhetoric. She highlighted the fact that eighteenth-century Scotland is literally an open book for scholars of rhetoric because the professors of the period published their lectures, lectures that are readily available in Scottish university archives. And in the last decade, much of this work has been reprinted in modern editions by Southern Illinois University Press, making eighteenth-century rhetoric accessible to researchers.

Win contributed to the expanding scholarship on eighteenth-century rhetoric by tracing the tremendous influence that these Scottish rhetoricians have had on American education, influence best shown by the use for almost a century of Hugh Blair's *Lectures on Rhetoric and Belles Lettres,* which was first published in 1783. Her bibliography, for a decade now, has introduced many graduate students to work in the history of rhetoric and has served as an essential resource for scholars in the field. Win also added to our understanding of the Scottish tradition by stressing the importance of George Jardine, a late eighteenth-century, early nineteenth-century Scottish rhetorician who helps to connect George Campbell and the eighteenth-century interest in epistemology with nineteenth-century Scottish rhetoricians like Alexander Bain, who was a major psychologist as well as an influential rhetorical theorist. Win's essay on this topic, "Rhetoric in the Liberal Arts: Nineteenth-Century Scottish Universities," also deepened our awareness of the broader educational trends that encouraged the Scots to introduce the study of English into higher education.

Win's most recent research has continued to follow the development of rhetoric and composition into the nineteenth century. In contrast to the rich scholarship in eighteenth-century rhetoric, nineteenth-century rhetoric had remained almost virtually closed to us because of a paucity of available materials. But Win has been instrumental in opening up the nineteenth century to further research. In the National Library of Scotland and in the Scottish university libraries, she discovered large collections of nineteenth-century notes on rhetoric, the bulk of these collections being sets of student notes from nineteenth-century courses in rhetoric. The importance of this discovery for rhetoric scholars goes without saying, but rich resources reside there as well for scholars in composition studies, cultural theory, and English literature because it was at this time and in this place that the study of composition, cultural theory, and English literature began as university disciplines. Indeed, even psychology and history as academic subjects had their historical beginnings in the courses in rhetoric and moral philosophy in the nineteenth-century Scottish universities. Before the discovery of these notes, these developments could not be traced. By searching out these notes and writing detailed descriptive annotations of them, Win has opened up rich material for other scholars and made this material readily available to American scholars. Out of this research has come Win's most recent book, *Nineteenth-Century Scottish Rhetoric: The American Connection* (Southern Illinois University Press, 1992).

These two books have given us valuable resources that will enrich our knowledge of rhetoric and composition for years to come. Rather than simply bringing a new perspective to a well-known field of study, Win has opened up areas of research for other students and scholars, a goal that she set for herself twenty years ago. That others are now beginning to work in the area of nineteenth-century Scottish rhetoric and thus to see its connection to contemporary research and teaching in literature and composition is not only the direct result of Win's work but also the strong confirmation that for us research is a shared activity in a community of scholars and teachers.

Composition Teaching and the Rediscovery of Rhetoric

Learning from our histories of rhetoric has enriched composition teaching. The rediscovery of the rhetorical tradition in English departments has resulted in valuable collections of primary readings, essays on theory and praxis, and bibliographic essays, which, along with our journals, have defined our area of study. Only in the last ten years have visionary editors and publishers like Kenney Withers of Southern Illinois University Press, Bob Boynton of Boynton/Cook, and Chuck Christensen of Bedford Books made it possible for people in rhetoric to add single-authored books, other than textbooks, to their contributions. For many years rhetorics and readers were the *sine qua non* for people in rhetoric, and such books did not count for much in promotion and tenure considerations, primarily because most members of promotion and tenure committees were literary scholars with expressed disdain for anything associated with teaching and for rhetoric, a metadiscipline that has practice as its very basis. Most of the many rhetorics published between the 1950s and 1980s show little evidence that histories and theories of rhetoric played any part in their conceptualization. (Indeed, underlying much of Robert J. Connors's history scholarship is the argument that one cannot understand composition studies today unless one knows the history of composition textbooks.) There are a few exceptions, stellar before-their-time textbooks, like Edward P.J. Corbett's *Classical Rhetoric for the Modern Student;* Richard Young, Alton Becker, and Kenneth Pike's *Rhetoric: Discovery and Change;* Frank J. D'Angelo's *Process and Thought in Composition;* Andrea Lunsford, Janice Lauer, Gene Montague, and Janet Emig's *Four Worlds of Writing*.

These textbooks were the practical vanguards of a new current in rhetorical theory that Kathleen Welch calls the "third generation of writing textbooks." She calls the former generation "boring" because these current-traditional textbooks "rely, whether they admit it or submerge it, on skill-bound writing instruction." Authors of these ahistorical and atheoretical textbooks fragment a *process* into sets of discrete skills, and "the student is then tutored in these skills." The idea behind such skill-driven books is that "the student writer will integrate these skills into her or his writing." But the third generation of textbooks goes beyond nonreflective, unchallenging texts. Although they may be "heavily theoretical," they "disguise their theory" (86). Although Welch marks *St. Martin's Guide to Writing* (Rise Axelrod and Charles Cooper) as the beginning of the third generation of rhetorics, Corbett, D'Angelo, and Young, Becker, and Pike provided beams of light in an otherwise dreary period of textbooks that emphasized correctness. Now we have other solid textbooks besides the "teacher-proof" *St. Martin's Guide*. Although most of them are more imitative than innovative compared to those mentioned above, they do achieve some compromise between the new and current-traditional rhetorics, thereby attracting many teachers who would not be drawn to a totally "new" textbook.

We need to keep in mind that only about thirty-five hundred college writing teachers out of over thirty-five thousand have professionalized themselves by learning the history, theory, and praxis of rhetoric, by participating in our national conferences, and by contributing to journals and professional books in rhetoric and composition. How brave then for Win to write—and St. Martin's Press to publish—a textbook for freshman writers, founded on classical rhetorical theory. *Rhetoric in the Classical Tradition* (1988) is structured clearly around the five classical canons and uses classical terminology. Ed Corbett's *Classical Rhetoric for the Modern Student* (1965) was aimed at freshman writers, but this venerable book, now in its third edition, for almost thirty years has been used primarily in advanced composition courses and, especially, graduate courses in rhetoric. Thus Win's *Rhetoric in the Classical Tradition* has carried on a tradition, being our only truly classical rhetoric for freshman of the nineties; this textbook has carried forward the third generation of rhetoric textbooks. Importantly, these books are scholarly in their own right; they have been influential in generating further research on using the histories of rhetoric.

Horner's Nontraditional Approach to the Study of Rhetoric

Although we recognize the value of Win's work in classical rhetoric, she is not a "classical rhetorician," at least in the sense of one who works in the original languages. Indeed, Win calls herself a "bootstrapper" because she is mostly self-trained in rhetoric, coming to it from a traditional concentration in literature and linguistics. Indeed, like all of our foremothers in rhetoric, Win's career has been nontraditional (see Crowley).

Win received her BA in English from Washington University in St. Louis, Missouri; then came marriage and children. When the oldest of her children was eleven, Win began her master's work in literature. With her MA at age 39, she taught part time at the University of Missouri, then became a full-time instructor. After she was tenured as an instructor in 1969, she worked for the director of composition, where, unrecognized and unrewarded, she did much of the work. In 1973, with full support from her family, she went to the University of Michigan for her doctoral work in English Language, Literature, and Linguistics. Studying with Richard Young, Alton Becker, Kenneth Pike, and Richard Enos, Win became interested in how we might learn from the history of rhetoric. In 1975, at fifty years of age and with her PhD in hand, she returned to Missouri as an assistant professor and began her seven-year tenure as director of composition. In 1980 she was promoted to associate professor, in 1984 to full professor.

Several converging factors during this time taught Win what, and who, she wanted to be in academia. Although the love and support of her family had sustained her for all these years, Win had no mentor. Although she was doing much of the composition director's work, she was given little respect for her administrative work. Although she created an exemplary training program for teaching assistants, the value of TA training was not recognized. Although she taught two courses in addition to virtually directing the program, running the TA preceptorship, and doing important research, she was not given recognition, respect, or compensation for bearing the sort of burdens that are all too familiar to many in rhetoric and composition, especially women.

Win made a conscious decision not to dwell on the inequities and personal attacks but, like the rhetorician she is, to bring about change, first in her own situation and then in the profession. She fought several battles against personal discrimination, including denial of her promotion to full professor. With determination she fought for the professional recognition that her department, like most traditional English departments, was reluctant to give to those working in rhetoric and composition.

Five times she filed grievances and argued her case before committees; five times she won.

Win is both a role model for and mentor to many of us, especially the women who make up the majority of those working in rhetoric and composition. Without the many kinds of support she has given to us victims of professionalized gender bias, we might not be the staunch but weary survivors some of us have become. Win has been formally recognized for her mentoring of women; the honor she's most proud of is being the 1982 recipient of the University of Missouri Alumnae Anniversary Award for Outstanding Contribution to the Education of Women. And at the 1991 Conference on College Composition and Communication, *Rhetoric Review* honored Win for the support she's given to so many women by naming the 1990–91 award for best essay "The Winifred Bryan Horner Award."

Horner has been tireless in her efforts to help women learn from events in her own academic history. We listen to, and heed, what she learned regarding the heavy administrative burdens placed especially on women when they should be doing research and writing. She scolds and cajoles—and we are the better for it. If you take on administrative work before tenure, she tells us, make sure it is in the agreement that one day a week—or two afternoons a week—you will not be in the office. This is your research time. Stick to it—whatever you do, do not even think you can work anywhere in the building where the composition office is. Do not even try to work at home. Go to the library. Hide, so no one can find you—and they will try. The "problem" will always be there in your office waiting for you the next morning.

For those of us in our forties and fifties who, like Win, have had nontraditional careers, usually coming to rhetoric from other disciplines or, like me, even other careers outside academia, she has been the mentor we never had in graduate school or in our own institutions. We have had to work harder because we started later than most. I remember when I first became aware of Win, at the 1983 4Cs meeting in Detroit. She appeared on a panel with Rich Enos and Jim Kinneavy: "Research in Historical Rhetoric." Afterward, I remember several of us who had been in the audience talking about her work; not knowing her academic history, we were puzzled that we had not known of her work before. One of our senior colleagues remarked that he had never heard of Winifred Bryan Horner until the year before. All of a sudden she just seemed to appear, he said, doing all this wonderful, scholarly, historical work in rhetoric. We too felt that way about this remarkable woman. She worked hard, establishing an extraordinary record at a later age than most scholars.

Alas, too many institutions—even some of our senior rhetoric scholars (males)—think starting late but doing the expected amount, or even more, of work in a specified time period is a disadvantage that works against women in promotion and tenure reviews. Horner has always regretted the time and emotional energy spent on fighting for deserved recognition and promotion, energy that could have been spent on legitimate research. Instead of deservedly receiving an institution's recognition and thanks for a nontraditional career and a concentrated record of scholarship in a short length of time, too often we receive just the opposite. One of our well-known senior scholars in rhetoric, who happens to be male and who shall be nameless, wrote as an outside reviewer for a female colleague's tenure review that her "late entry" into the profession had "undoubtedly slowed [her] down." I know of others, women especially, who have been victims of discrimination, intended or not, because they have had nontraditional academic careers. It seems to matter not that many of these women have published as much or more as others, especially males, who are being promoted to associate professors with tenure at various institutions across the country. Win has taught us how to fight such discrimination more effectively by channeling our anger into scholarly activity. Many of us women in rhetoric and composition who have benefited from her personal and professional support are forging ahead with our academic careers and fighting for our rightful places as scholars.

Writing the Future by Rewriting the History of Rhetoric

Though Win is secure now, and receiving deserved honors such as this festschrift and the first twentieth-century chair in rhetoric awarded to a woman (the Lillian Radford Chair of Rhetoric and Composition at Texas Christian University), she would be the first to say that although we are winning more battles, we must not stop the fight, ever. Indeed, added to the professional problems both men and women in rhetoric and composition have encountered are ominous clouds that have brought increasing controversy over the ongoing theory and practice debate. But this is not the old debate on "bridging the gap" between literature and composition, the subject of another well-received book by Win. As rhetoric continues to manifest its metadisciplinary nature (e.g., recent work shows how poststructuralists use rhetoric to create and sustain their own theoretical domains), those who consider themselves "compositionists" but not "rhetoricians" are talking of secession. In the meeting rooms and hallways at 4Cs, we are increasingly hearing how the recent emphasis on "theory" is making those who emphasize "practice" feel marginalized. What makes this debate uncomfortable for so many of us is its similarity to the separate, armed camps of literature and composition so prevalent in English departments of the 1980s. In the nineties we find the factions within our own community that we have fought so hard to form and legitimate.

This book has come out of concern that the conjunctive in "rhetoric and composition" will be replaced by a disjunctive. Rhetoric and composition are not really even two sides of the same coin. The special nature of rhetoric and composition is that it theorizes practice and applies theory as its central act. It has been no different since Aristotle conceptualized what was effective in the ways human beings use language. We need to learn from our histories of rhetoric, as Don Stewart has urged us again and again, so that we can use this knowledge to draw rhetoric and composition together, to understand theory in practice and the practice of theory as they were conceptualized in ancient times.

In the sixties and seventies, we needed to know our history. Unlike other areas of study, our teaching was not often based on the knowledge of rhetoric as a substantive art with its own body of knowledge but on rhetoric as a methodology only. Thus we worked too often not as a community of teacher scholars drawn together by a sense of our history but as discoverers of a "brand new world every morning" (Bryant). Now that we have gone through that process, we recognize how histories of rhetoric have defined our field of study. We have rediscovered the rhetorical tradition; now we need to redefine what we do in light of our deepening and broadening understanding of rhetoric. What we can begin to do more effectively is to use our knowledge of history by intelligently incorporating it into our teaching of writing. This volume of essays by Win's friends and colleagues I hope will generate further work in learning from the histories of rhetoric. The collection honors Winifred Bryan Horner for her sustained work in teaching us how we ourselves can honor and learn from our past, and use it on our way toward becoming better teachers.

Works Cited

Bryant, Paul T. "A Brand New World Every Morning." *College Composition and Communication* 25 (1974): 30–33.

Crowley, Sharon. "Three Heroines: An Oral History." *PRE/TEXT* 9 (1988): 202–06.

Welch, Kathleen E. *The Contemporary Reception of Classical Rhetoric: Appropriations of Ancient Discourse.* Hillsdale, NJ: Lawrence Erlbaum Associates, 1990.

Part 1

Studying the Histories of Rhetoric

▼

2 *Using the History of Rhetoric*

Richard Lloyd-Jones

When I first met History in School, I learned that I was not and never would be an Historian. The teacher said that one studied History for its own sake, because it was a pleasure in itself, not because it was useful. I liked study for its own sake even then, but I distrusted his way of speaking. I wish he had meant that it was liberating learning, not servile knowledge, but his examinations showed such a preoccupation with isolated "facts" that he seemed sincere in claiming that one studied History for itself alone. The "facts" of his world were random— although he liked to have each one dated and filed serially—and were justified by their mere existence.

In a way I did not mind because I ignored him, liked the stories of history, and made little effort to separate history from myth or fiction. All were written narratives, and each in its way enchanted me. Eventually I came to understand that the story, the interpretation, not the facts in themselves, was what gathered me in. The facts were merely the hooks on which one strung the multicolored threads that make up a life. The more hooks, the more complex and exciting the weave, but still the fun was in the story and the truth was in the revealed relationships among the hooks. Given facts, albeit never all of the facts, a skilled weaver could thread many stories, each a version of truth appropriate for storms or blinding sun, for gentle breezes or pelting rain. I dismissed the teachers of History and read history as I happened upon it.

Fortunately one may live long enough to change one's mind. I met revisionists who discovered forgotten facts, or emphasized facts that had been suppressed, and thus I found that even historians can make new stories. Those teachers who frowned when I interpreted their daily dole of facts in my peculiar way had been hiding inconvenient information, and I welcomed those scholars who enriched the body of fact so I could justify new stories with more elaborate patterns of hooks. In this way history was a pleasure in itself, as are other kinds of fiction, things made of words, so then even History was for me officially open to discovery. Play with words invites rearranging the mind.

Alas, I soon learned that these discoverers and interpreters of New Facts were as set in their ways as were my first teachers. For them the American Revolution had six causes — six and six only. Romantics were children of Nature; city-bred people who hated walks in the woods could not be Romantics. All changes of societies were rooted in economic forces. These people saw only one set of connections among their Facts, one kind of orthodoxy. I was simply expected to acquire more complicated lists to memorize.

The tenor of our time is reductionist and categorical and hierarchical, so I suppose it is to be expected that some histo-rians, too, want life to be tidy and neat so that it can be explained in fifty-minute hours and tested on multiple choice forms. If *Cliff's Notes* or Lamb's *Shakespeare* substitute for the originals, why not reduce history to the abstractions the facts are supposed to anchor? I had reviled Gradgrind and McChokumchild and their celebration of "fact" as Dickens portrayed them in *Hard Times* only to find that interpreters, users, of history made the past simply into a tool of their persuasion, Rhetoric as Aristotle had defined it. I probably would not have minded if they had allowed me to use the received facts to fashion my own myths for my time.

Indeed, about the propriety of Rhetoric I had no doubts. My mind was as set toward social effect as the minds of those who required their own interpretations. I had learned from the Greeks via high school debate that Rhetoric was a useful art, that one learned from Rhetoricians how to persuade in public situa-tions to gain support for the common good, an essential element of responsible government. "Let us debate according to the rules, and we'll have wise policies." Eventually I would learn that Rhetoric was also useful in assessing probability, in identifying contingent truths that make up so much of our uncertain lives. In our practical innocence we spoke of "our" devices of discourse and of "their" tricks of argument, but we knew our scholastic goals were to master the crafts of language. Eventually—years later—I heard of Isocrates and learned that our sophistry was neither new nor entirely irresponsible. To be sure, for centuries one kind of historian had made sophists into amoralists, but perhaps any absolutist classifies any kind of agnostic as amoral. We may have learned our practical rules of debate from second-hand Aristotle, but our sense of reality was rooted in another classical tradition—humans are the measure of all things.

Still, I believe I fortified my concern for technique in high school Latin. I learned versification and much about literary tropes as I inched through the *Aeneid*. Like other beginners with alien languages we read the story as though it were all written in super-slow motion, considering the social behavior of the actors, the tricks of grammar, the modern derivatives of the words, and the design of phrases. As we deconstructed without knowing it, we learned for sure that Virgil had made the poem with mortal craft, had a pious purpose in his design, and revealed the workings of his craft so that other wordsmiths could follow.

But it was Cicero who made me understand the rhetorical craftiness of Virgil as well as the rhetorical dimension of all literature. We read only the orations—again it was years later before I read Cicero's explicit teaching—but close analysis convinced us of rhetorical design. I loved his accusations made in the guise of dismissing them, and the wonderful drama of Latin word order—"To death, Cataline . . ." By graduate school to me the amplifications of sixteenth- and seventeenth-century English prose seemed natural, as did the often-rehearsed structure of the oration, and I thought I could understand the Ciceronian style without even reading the commentaries of Cicero or his contemporaries. My mild excursion into Renaissance prose was at most secondhand classicism, but I was enlightened by the historical studies of others.

In my fool's errand I soon took up teaching, and I resolved not to be a teacher of History. In the first place I was training to teach Literature, and more or less accepted the grandeur of that calling as described in the New Criticism, but even then I realized that rhetoric, the art of persuasion, the practical art, is also primarily the practical art of teaching, that informing is the art of persuading a listener to hear and see and do as you hear and see and do. One does not change a mind already made up, but one shapes unconsidered perceptions into meaning. One makes reality imaginable by representing it in discourse. Nay more, by pressing students to represent what they sense, a teacher guides them to understand the stories that bind us together in a society. I have never been very successful in separating Literature and Rhetoric, even when I pretended to literary criticism. We are first what our stories make us out to be, and only then what our serried categories summarize of experience, but perhaps I should build a bridge across this chasm over which my imagination vaulted.

You may guess rightly that I had been led into semiotics. Philosopher Hubert Alexander introduced me to the serious study of language by way of Charles Morris, and a host of Speech teachers offered General Semantics, and Speech Therapists slipped in both linguistics and psychology, so I could easily have become an ahistorical theorist. As an undergraduate I was taken by these grand systems, although in truth I still spoke of myself as a poet, a crafty poet, and used these language theorists to guide my study of prosody and poetics. I did not become a Philosopher of Language any more than I became an Historian; I simply absorbed their insights.

I was saved from academic pretension by my initiation into teaching. My first students were juniors and seniors in business and engineering, and they wanted my high school Aristotle recast into prescriptions to fit their cases. They lived quite comfortably without History or history. I had grown up in the world of small-town business, learning to give the customer what he or she wants, and anyway, in one's first semester of teaching one teaches whatever one can, so watered Aristotle they had. Dressed in modern jargon, too.

I do not pretend that decoration with ancient precedents is any reason to study the history of rhetoric, and at that point I really had not done so. But the ancient rules were grounded in public practice not so far removed from modern business as we might prefer to believe. The rational surfaces, then and now, sometimes hide barbaric coercion. The ancient epistemology we doubtless have replaced; that is why Knobloch and Brannon get so upset about our using classical rhetoric, for they imply that accepting the surface commits us to the foundations as well. I doubt that.

Practical decisions do not commit us to absolute consistency in our theoretical models. Learned folks also have created wild theories about the subatomic structure of physical things, and their theories give us power to create astonishing technologies, but most of us in our practical lives can and do survive on Aristotle's physics. Or Ptolemy's. The new theories serve experts practically in shooting for the moon, but for most of us they change our public sense of reality only superficially. Most of the time we understand the world in terms the Greeks could understand. We accept old theories and new ones simultaneously, even when they are in conflict. In fact, most of us are comfortable with a handful of conflicting theories because we are adept in choosing the one that helps us attend to our current needs.

If History explains to us how our sense of what is real has changed, at least when we are pretending to be learned, then surely it is liberating as well as fun. Maybe it is fun because it is liberating. We learn to live with inconsistency and to make judgments about which story is useful for explaining what we need to understand now. When we teach History in school, it may well be fun, but we also use it to shape the understanding of the young, presumably because such shaping allows them to learn how theories are related to time and place, itself a liberating notion, and liberation is a social good. We are not so much following Patrick Henry in having our feet guided by History as we are considering relationships between material transience and enduring patterns. We are helping youngsters define themselves within complex societies and among alternative complex societies in a very mobile world.

Within that broad view of the use of history, the history of rhetoric is especially compelling although often overlooked.

One can measure an age (or place) tellingly by identifying its theories of discourse as well as its practice of discourse. A teacher notes that in both Greece and Rome the theorists were teachers who took active part in public affairs. On the side they speculated about the nature of truth and knowledge, the necessary content of their persuasive messages, but they were interested in social results. Who was guilty of what? What policy should the state follow? Who or what is worthy of emulation? These are questions of how people relate to each other. The answers suggest how a family becomes a tribe becomes a state becomes an empire. They are still overwhelming questions.

When the Church took over Rhetoric, the underlying issue was to make Truth-bearing texts intelligible and attractive to the common person. When Chaucer's Pardoner told us that ordinary people like stories, he was not asserting that narrative is a key source of knowledge, as we might, but that stories can be fashioned so as to make the Church's teachings fit into experience. One might argue that ancient dialectic primarily explored the meaning of statements in order to discover Truth and thus could not be expected to deliver "new" knowledge, but the Truth of the middle ages was explicitly delivered in Text and needed delivery in common discourse rather than discovery. Renaissance rhetoricians in reasserting the human role in judging "all things" retained the stylistic machinery of earlier eras, found courtliness an adequate replacement for assured Truth. The elegant animalism of courtly behavior ensured individual survival within the re-forming states of Europe, but it also redefined both individual and society.

Condensing two millenia into a paragraph is a kind of lie, the sort teachers offer to provide "context" in a class really devoted to examining detailed studies of limited scope. But it also is a corrective for another kind of lie that governs "how-to" courses in writing. Systems of advice about discourse are not neutral; individuals and societies have axes to grind. I am not denouncing an evil; I merely am reporting an attribute of humans—people see and do as they understand their needs. That we now can praise liberating arts as well as useful ones simply tells what comfortable animals some of us are. We can afford to think of the free play of mind, of symbols, of "selfless" aspiration. One could hardly have writing courses devoted to finding or exploring the self if external social needs were not already comfortably cared for. Because individual students are often primarily concerned with what writing will be required in their own fields, whether in college or later, they are sometimes happier with "practical" courses.

Place as well as time determines both ends and means in rhetorical systems. For example, we argue that education in global affairs is essential because we must deal with people not like us. We have accepted—at least some of us have—that world trade and electronic communications, wars and wanderings, and even overcrowded populations make understanding and communicating with alien cultures on the planet now essential to survival. We are constantly reminded that peaceful persuasive techniques in one culture do not necessarily work in another, so impatient people talk of weapons and power when they ought to study how other cultures have solved problems of mortal conflict. To restrain our eagerness for short-term coercive success by imposing our social will in favor of long-term cooperative accommodations designed to allow unlike people to live together seems essential. Yet every attempt to revise curricula so as to challenge our traditional sense of reality and value encounters prophecies of our cultural collapse. In the United States, a veritable market place of cultural traditions, teaching about cultural diversity seems necessary if we are to preserve the nation itself, but that requires us to compare theories of rhetoric rather than to master formulas of discourse.

The irony of these observations is that a quick view of the history of rhetoric shows that the "tradition" exhibits notable cultural diversity, too. Each innovator redefined the cultural landscape, noted new social pressures, accepted different notions of truth, observed new combinations of anxieties, and slightly recast the "old" rules. Often the same terms were used, but slightly skewed, and created the illusion of sameness. Anyway, the believers in the "old Truth" died and ceased to be threats to survival, even though young mossbacks may have espoused oddly misshapen versions of old systems. They simply become part of the chorus of diverse cultures that are always present and insistently challenge the authority of whoever is currently powerful.

In our time we may have to do something about the Chinese or the Iranians or the Angolans, and so we concede we have to know how they persuade themselves of policy, but we sometimes think we can simply ignore Augustine or Ramus or Fred Newton Scott. Still, each of the older rhetoricians is potentially a threat to our way of thinking. That we may have "derived" from them merely distracts us from examining what is the real basis of their beliefs and ours. We prefer to use history to tell us that we are the same as our ancestors when we should also note that in crucial ways we are different.

These are arguments about the value of history for students of culture and perhaps for philosophers, but what about student writers? Why shouldn't they be satisfied with handbooks up-dated to serve a global society? I can thank many who helped me as a classroom teacher resee the old boys so I could be a better writing coach—Kenneth Burke, Ross Winterowd, Ed Corbett, Kathleen Welch, Bill Irmscher, Jerry Murphy, Ellen Quandahl, Mike Halloran, and many others. Your list would doubtless be different, for there is not a clear canon of commentators. I am perhaps even more taken by lessons from Win Horner, Don Stewart, Walker Gibson, Jim Berlin, John Brereton, Ann Berthoff, Carl Klaus, Sam Watson, and others who introduced me to people I had never heard of. Their preoccupations remind me of the arbitrariness of choice in making histories and gave me new hooks for my threads. I am grateful for what these scholars have learned and have taught to me, but have they made me a more useful teacher? How much of what they have said do I pass on to whom?

Rhetoric remains a practical art. No matter how exotic the theory, the discussion resolves itself into practical choices about what bit of language to use when. The theories establish ends, standards of judgment, but they explain the ends and standards in examples fit for their time and place, and they establish the grounds from which my own standards emerge. As a crafter I learn from craft, and I coach those who would also master the craft. When I teach Plato, I argue his craft even more than his overt message. Even in translation the text lives as an example of discourse, but I still read Plato better, help my students read better, for my having read the commentaries, the histories. With their help I can better imagine situations beyond the ones of my daily life and thus am alert to a broader range of devices. I experience discourse, and I know about discourse through practice. But to understand what is going on I need a sense of theory evolving within a context.

What is good for the teacher is good for the student, but time and spirit are finite, so the apology goes. A beginner has so much to learn. Making rough sense in daily life is a reasonable goal for most people in most classes. On the other hand, even though a touch of theory for awareness, an ancient analog for spice, and a countering example to discourage overgeneralization may be all the practical engineering student can tolerate, some flavor of liberation is crucial in even the most servile course if one is to learn about adaptation to the unexpected.

The teacher—actual or potential—needs a sense of irony about craft and usefulness in order to be truly crafty and useful, and that requires excursions into history. Teaching composition by formula, as many handbooks do, is inevitably self-defeating. The here-and-now formula is, alas, only for here-and-now, but this afternoon something is different from what happened in the morning. As an administrator I wrote formula letters and kept a supply of boilerplate in the computer to fill out quickly many standard responses. That was practical in a gross world where subtle distinctions are irrelevant and time is short, but it invited one to ignore change, to overgeneralize. Trainers, like spell-checkers, do better with fewer options, but teachers must always seek another way. The historians as I now understand them are people who collect "other ways" tried in other times.

The materials in a book like this one will be used many ways but perhaps the extremes of adaptation will illustrate the need for them. For potential teachers and scholars we offer courses in rhetorical theory that are parallel to courses in literary criticism. Some deal in history, some deal in particular problems or categories.

Those who will be researchers in Rhetoric like those who seek to be researchers of Literature attempt to "master" the "whole" body of theory even as they quietly overlook or ignore what they cannot find or have not time to find. The scholars of this book, those like Win Horner, offer information to fill the "holes" in their learning. Those who are primarily teachers—or perhaps are literary scholars who must teach composition occasionally—depend on such writings for defensive reasons, to avoid saying stupid things about language and society, but also for guidance. They must choose among competing theories, make sense of textbooks and shorthand advice about writing, and so need the standard graduate course. Literary scholars sometimes claim that graduate students can acquire all of the critical theory they need in the context of advanced courses in literature, but so few really advanced courses in writing exist that a parallel claim cannot be made for rhetoric. Furthermore, we have had a long hiatus from the serious study of nonfiction prose and rhetorical theory and history, so few teachers of writing have a good sense of context. Even the most elementary knowledge cannot be taken for granted, so they cannot make brief allusions designed to reactivate knowledge acquired somewhere else. Yet, the design of courses is easy once rhetorical texts are obtained because the course pattern is a familiar one.

The difficult challenge for those concerned with historical perspective is to offer it to students who are mystified by language and afraid of error, those frozen by formulas into stilted and often inappropriate phrases. They write like Frankenstein's monster walked, and they need larger views of human relationships. Perhaps Miss Manners can help, perhaps traditional grammar and modern linguistics help those with a scientific bent, perhaps the self-discovery courses offer boosts to confidence, but I suspect all approaches are improved when they are laced with the spirit of history, the sense of changing context. True, my classroom allusion to Plato, or Ramus, or Bain, or Horner may be a mere analog to the TV appeals to the authority of an athlete in attesting to a soft drink, but they also—with a few extra words— may suggest how different people in different times arranged their worlds and solved their problems. A word or two more may even suggest how the old solution defines our sense of the new problem. Just how is the TV appeal to authority like or different from the classical one?

Writing, like other crafts, is passed on by imitation and coaching. Nowadays we coach most often in small groups, so we enlist the several experiences in the group for additional commentaries, one writer to another. We may call the group an editorial conference or a class, and we may have quite specific tasks to do or simply react to whatever texts fledgling writers bring to us, but for a time we make ourselves into appropriate audiences and offer reactions. The principal coach, who has experienced the most writing and has examined the broadest range of theories about discourse, issues challenges that will evoke from students revealing attempts to control language and lead to discovery about discourse, but even that person must in the end explain. The students' experience needs interpretation. Why this task? Why did people react to the solution this way? What is implied in other responses to the challenge?

An answer couched entirely in terms of modern psychology and sociology and lingusitics is doubtless possible, but I suspect such modern answers are overly certain. The language of science is pridefully definite. I would rather have the openended promises of historical allusion, of rules defined in time and space with limited applications. It is not so tidy, but it may be more useful. These three-minute stories and five-minute lectures serve mechanically as classroom transitions from student paper to student paper, but they also tie student papers to human wisdom of the past. In that they redefine the student.

3 Reinventing Rhetorical Traditions

Thomas P. Miller

The rhetorical tradition is a fiction that has just about outlasted its usefulness. Composition specialists have used the prestige of a classical heritage to make the teaching of writing respectable in English departments, but only a new discipline speaks of its past as "the tradition" because such a univocal and unproblematic sense of history loses its currency when people create competing traditions for the field, as is currently being done. Unfortunately, emerging disciplines often turn from valorizing the tradition to vilifying it, as is evident in the efforts to blame the current-traditional paradigm on everyone from Aristotle to eighteenth-century commonsense philosophers.

If we could move beyond honoring and condemning the rhetorical tradition, we might be able to develop a more dynamic relationship between historical inquiry and contemporary theory and practice. Instead of just the rhetorical tradition, we need to study the rhetoric of traditions—the ways that political parties, ethnic groups, social movements, and other discourse communities constitute and maintain the shared values and assumptions that authorize discourse. If we adopt this more broadly engaged approach, we can begin to make the discursive practices of marginalized traditions a central part of the history of rhetoric, and the history of rhetoric will then become more central to our interest in rhetoric as a social praxis.

Such a redefinition of the rhetorical tradition is hardly a radical innovation. The accepted canon includes practical political speeches by Isocrates and Demosthenes alongside the theories of Aristotle, but such inclusions are part of the received tradition and have not been used to add nontraditional practitioners of the arts of rhetoric. Given the constitution of the canon, one must conclude that for a couple of thousand years the only people who used rhetoric were white male Europeans, a state of affairs that is at odds with our belief that every community uses rhetoric to put shared assumptions and values into social practice.

Our failure to challenge the canon is surprising because we work in departments that are deeply involved with canonization.[1] Unlike our literature colleagues, we have only recently discovered that we have a canon, and we have busily put it to use to establish graduate programs and professionalize composition. Through graduate seminars, doctoral reading lists, and a shared body of historical scholarship, we have institutionalized the rhetorical tradition as a basic part of rhetoric and composition. We have succeeded in making the rhetorical tradition something to be studied, taught, and tested. Perhaps we ought to ask if it actually exists, or at least if it is the only story we need to be telling ourselves about our past. If we can set aside the idea of a unified rhetorical tradition of canonical texts, we may be able to take a broader perspective that makes rhetorical processes like canonization the object of historical study. But how then can we reinvent the rhetorical tradition in terms of the rhetoric of traditions?

We can start by admitting that the rhetorical tradition is a fiction, and a rather strained one at that. To write Demosthenes, Augustine, Ramus, Campbell, and Burke (Kenneth or Edmund) into the same history, we have to ignore, or at least simplify, the complex differences between their political, intellectual, and educational contexts. Otherwise, the abstract continuities the story depends on will be lost in the details of specific situations. We have to pretend that when figures like Isocrates and Ramus talk about rhetoric, they are talking about the same thing. Of course we try to locate this thing in different historical contexts, but I doubt that I am alone in feeling how inadequately those differences get conveyed in a lecture on civic humanism or a discussion of a chapter from Ong. Most of our seminars (and the research that informs them) cannot locate the history of rhetoric in the context of changing educational and political practices in more than a cursory fashion. When we write essays that explain a century of composition studies, or survey two thousand years of rhetorics in a course or two, we cannot adequately attend to the purposeful responses to practical situations that make rhetoric rhetorical. This process of abstracting texts from their rhetorical contexts is often tacitly adopted from the new critics and historians of ideas who taught most of us. However, if we want to prepare students to do more than reread the history of ideas about rhetoric, then we need to teach and study history more like rhetoricians and less like philosophers or literary critics. What would that mean? What would be involved in developing a rhetorical perspective on the history of rhetoric?

Questions about the rhetorical tradition and traditional ways of studying rhetoric have to be asked together because we need to do more than read old books in new ways or read new books in old ways if we want to revitalize the relationship between historical scholarship and current theory and practice. Because we are located in departments dedicated to the interpretation of texts, we have concentrated on interpreting canonical texts and have written almost no social histories of rhetoric and composition. Despite our professed interest in teaching, very little research has been done on the history of instruction, with virtually no one doing archival research in either the traditional or Foucaultian senses of archive.[2] Our historical research has been shaped by the model of literary studies: The task is generally defined as developing a new reading of a classic text, perhaps consulting some historical research but rarely making a concerted effort to document the socioinstitutional context or the broader historical formation in which the text was situated.

The model of the critic in a library with a good book and the MLA bibliography is not a bad paradigm, but we need to do other kinds of research if we want to get more texts on the table. We need to do more field work, the sort of digging into educational and social practices that Winifred Horner has often called "spade work." I am not suggesting we can dig down to the facts themselves or that the contexts of a text are any less problematic or more open to interpretation than the text itself is. I do think, however, that we need to look beyond the literary theories that have gained prestige in English departments to combine a broader historicism with our own developing understanding of rhetoric as a social praxis.

Historians in many fields have established two complementary sorts of research programs: local histories that provide detailed descriptions of the cultural experiences of specific communities, and more global accounts of historical formations that locate discursive practices in the context of existing social relations, institutional structures, and dominant ideologies. Both of these sorts of research can help us to develop a rhetorical perspective on the history of rhetoric, as I would like to show by sketching out an example of each.

Historians in diverse fields are moving beyond rereading the canonical texts of elite traditions to develop richly detailed descriptions of the shared experiences of local communities, often in the assumption that popular cultural forms like chapbooks and community festivals challenge the authority of the dominant discourse and create a space for the expression of suppressed traditions.[3] The emphasis on "thick descriptions" of specific contexts is compatible with rhetoric's traditional concern for the situational nature of discourse and with the current awareness that to understand functional literacy, one must know the social contexts in which it functions. What ethnographers like Geertz have termed *local knowledge* includes the shared experiences and values of a community, knowledge that rhetoricians must use to show that they speak for the group. Rhetoricians justify their positions by locating them in the shared traditions of the group. To speak for the group, they must invent a discourse authorized by the shared traditions. To understand this social process, we must try to reinvent the traditions within and against which the rhetorician worked, traditions that may have been silenced by the dominant discourse. While we can never step into the "native's point of view," we need to know more about the values, experiences, and assumptions shared by specific communities if we want to understand their characteristic rhetorical practices.

One site for this sort of localized historical research is the women's academies that became common in the eighteenth century. By 1798 Judith Sargent Murray could write that "female academies are every where establishing" because of "the establishment of the female intellect" (qtd. in Kerber 221). These academies went beyond the learning appropriate for the kitchen, drawing room, and nursery to encompass a range of subjects that included English literature and composition. The academies used textbooks like *The Young Ladies' Miscellany* (1723) by Daniel Bellamy and *Letters to a Young Lady on a Course of English Poetry* by John Aikin. Aikin was Priestley's predecessor as tutor of Belles Lettres and Languages in the Dissenting academy at Warrington from 1757 to 1761. Aikin has been called "the first systematic lecturer in English Literature" by George Saintsbury (qtd. in Turner ii).

What were the differences between the teaching of English in women's and men's academies? What attitudes and experiences were engendered in those differences, and how did they affect the ways women read and wrote? Did these academies help to publicize women's discourse in the way that becomes observable in the period? Over three hundred titles by and about women were published in America between 1750 and 1810 according to Evans's bibliography, and they are widely available in the microcard collection that parallels the bibliography, though few people in rhetoric and composition take advantage of such archives.[4] This women's reading public is evident in the genre of women's novels that included Richardson's *Pamela,* which presents a model writer who educated herself by reading Locke. Important archival sources also include self-improvement works like Steele's *The Ladies Library* (1714) and periodicals like *Ladies Mercury* (1693), *The Female Tatler* (1709), and *Female Spectator* (1744).

At a time when educated women were satirized in print and discouraged by most communities, the Dissenters were notable for encouraging women's education. Traditional sources of female literacy will become more evident as we develop a detailed understanding of the experience of literate women and the social constraints they lived within. It is significant that in America, and probably elsewhere, a woman's level of literacy was less dependent on the educational or social background of her parents than on whether they were regular churchgoers (Graff 164–65).

Radicals like Mary Wollstonecraft were Dissenters, but Dissenters also included conservative evangelists like Hannah Moore. Moore was a Methodist, and it was the Methodists who did more to promote working-class literacy than any other group (Altick 35). In reaction to the political unrest spread by the unprecedented popularity of the writings of Thomas Paine (who was also educated by Dissenters), Moore consciously imitated popular chapbooks to write moralizing tales intended to make sure that increased literacy did not lead to increased political activism.[5] Rhetoricians like Wollstonecraft and Moore need to be written into a rhetorical tradition, as do women like Laetitia Anna Aikin Barbauld, Aikin's daughter and Priestley's student. Barbauld was a well-known critic, poet, religious and political writer, and teacher and advocate of Rousseau's educational philosophy. Some of her writings are related to our traditional interests, including an edition of the *Spectator,* a collection of Richardson's letters with a biography and critical account of his writings, political pamphlets like *An Address to the Opposers of the Repeal of the Corporation and Test Acts* (1790), and *The Female Speaker* (1811).

When we look beyond the rhetorical tradition, we will discover many such rhetorical traditions. To reinvent such traditions, we need localized accounts of the shared experiences of the community as well as more broadly focused research on discursive practices, social conventions, material conditions, and political ideologies. To provide an example of how research on broader historical formations can help us to reinvent rhetorical traditions, I will use some concepts of Bakhtin and Gramsci to suggest how the expansion of the reading public in the eighteenth century contributed to the constitution of college English studies. We have come to accept that college English studies began in the nineteenth century, when a scholarly discipline appeared that begins to look like what English departments do today. However, English composition, rhetoric, and literature were widely taught in eighteenth-century colleges (see Miller).

If we are serious about teaching, we need to take teaching seriously as a sociohistorical practice and treat the classroom as a scene of historical change, a project that is well suited to the sort of localized research already discussed. We also need to take a broader perspective to examine how English was constituted as an object of study by social changes that made the contemporary idiom problematic enough to merit study. In the process of their formation, disciplines respond directly to the intellectual and political forces that tend to become internalized when the discipline has achieved apparent autonomy.

In the last half of the eighteenth century, English was widely taught at the college level by Scots, Dissenters, and Americans. The same trends that institutionalized English studies in the British cultural provinces led to efforts to regulate public usage like Johnson's dictionary and hundreds of grammars, rhetorics, and treatises on language. After centuries of comparative neglect, what had happened to make English problematic enough to merit such widespread attention? In the last half of the eighteenth century, the annual publication of books almost quadrupled, with the number of novels published annually growing from seven to forty and the number of newspapers sold doubling from midcentury to 1780 (Watts 37, 290; Altick 48). Print was becoming a public presence of unprecedented economic and political significance. With the explosion of periodicals, histories, translations, novels, and cheap reprints of traditional literary and scholarly works, educated culture was no longer the domain of courtly patrons and learned scholars (see Eagleton). Several factors served to publicize literature and learning: Books became cheaper and more widely available, the vernacular became the language of learning and culture as well as commerce and politics, and literacy spread to a broader social sphere, both in terms of a broader range of social classes and a wider domain of socioeconomic experience. The popularization and commercialization of literacy created a state of what Bakhtin has called *heteroglossia,* a state of discourse with many voices and few borders. Grammarians and rhetoricians set out to map those borders, legislate the laws that governed the domain of polite discourse, and thus regulate access to it. College English studies were part of this broad social process.

We need to develop models of intellectual and social change that can help us to study the rhetorical processes that connect the two. The constitution of English as an object of study was shaped by the dialectical interaction of what Bakhtin has termed the *centrifugal* and *centripetal forces* in discourse—the movement outward to include more diverse voices in the cultural dialogue and the contrary tendency to establish regularities to try to make discourse univocal (67, 269–72). Bakhtin considers the novel to be the "dialogic" genre, and according to Watt, the realistic narrative form of the novel was first conventionalized by such eighteenth-century writers as Defoe, who was one of the first students of college English (Miller). Bakhtin has proven to be a valuable source for the sort of localized research already discussed, but the work of Gramsci can also help us to study the rhetorical dimensions of social change. Unlike traditional Marxists, Gramsci argues that social change is not determined by economics because most dominant groups exercise a cultural hegemony based in a broad consensus and not simply in economic power (see Adamson and Salamini). To achieve hegemony, a group must produce intellectuals who can formulate and promote the ideologies that unify an emerging class and authorize its broader influence. Intellectuals play a vital role in the process of constituting and maintaining hegemony, which is a rhetorical process because groups that depend on authoritarian control or violence are weak and unstable and may soon be replaced by other emerging groups.

Gramsci's analysis of intellectuals defines sites for research on how rhetoric promotes social cohesion and change (see *Prison Notebooks* 5–14). For Gramsci, everyone can be an intellectual because all people use their intellect to solve problems, interpret experience, and express themselves. Intellectuals are defined not by anything intrinsic to what they do, but by the roles they play in social groups. Two types of intellectuals can be distinguished by the ways they function in social groups. *Organic* intellectuals aid in the formation of a group by articulating shared experiences, values, and objectives. *Traditional* intellectuals are produced by previous historical developments and claim a false autonomy from current class interests. Organic intellectuals are directly engaged with the practical work of a social group, while traditional intellectuals often fill professional roles that give them an apparent economic independence. Gramsci frequently cites clergy as the best example of traditional intellectuals because they claim the independent authority of a sacred heritage but have historically strengthened the hegemony of established elites. As an example of organic intellectuals, Gramsci cites specialists in business and industrial technology who help to articulate and maintain the hegemony of the urban bourgeoisie. Such hegemony was achieved by gaining a broad consensual support for the cultural values and social programs of the middle classes, and not just by nature of their roles as managers of the modes of production.

Gramsci defines intellectuals as rhetoricians who articulate the shared interest of social groups, thus enabling rising classes to achieve hegemony. Organic intellectuals have a dialectical relationship to social practice: they create shared understanding, and their practical understanding depends on their engagement with the experience of the group. If this engagement is lost, they become traditional intellectuals and will end up serving other classes. Gramsci creates a dialectical relationship between intellectual and social change that is fundamental to understanding rhetoric as a social praxis. We need to develop programs of historical research centered on questions about this dialectical relationship. We need to ask who speaks through a particular rhetorician (a complicated question because leaders of marginalized groups are often coopted and come to speak for the existing hegemony). How does rhetoric help to create group identity and transform shared values into practical action toward common goals? And how is the formation of social groups shaped by broader hegemonic forces, including existing economic conditions, political relations, and dominant ideologies?

Gramsci shared our interest in such questions because he knew that language inscribed changing social relations.

> [E]very time the question of the language surfaces, in one way or another, it means that a series of other problems are coming to the fore: the formation and enlargement of the governing class, the need to establish more intimate and secure relationships between the governing groups and the national-popular mass, in other

words to reorganize the cultural hegemony. (*Cultural Writings* 183–84)

Such a reorganization of cultural hegemony led to the constitution of English as an object of study. The introduction of college English studies was but one part of the intellectual developments that would come to justify the hegemony of the middle classes, developments as diverse as capitalist political economics, theories of personal morality that based ethical standards in the feelings of individuals, utilitarian philosophies of social governance, applied experimental research, and belletristic cultural theories that helped the middle classes to understand themselves as a class. Such apparently unconnected developments were initiated by the same intellectuals who introduced English studies and made them the characteristic concern of the polite reading public. Adam Smith, Joseph Priestley, and Hugh Blair were not just three of the first college teachers of English; they were public intellectuals whose works helped to constitute the middle-class reading public as a hegemonic force.

The reorganization of cultural hegemony can clearly be seen in the formation of the middle-class reading public. A diverse body of research shows that the reading public for secular periodicals and books was expanding to include the middle classes, as well as the sort of literate workers who would become the organic intellectuals of working-class political movements at the turn of the century (see Altick, Lacquer, and Thompson). Increased social mobility encouraged people to believe that they could improve their station by emulating the taste and usage of their betters. Such attitudes promoted the production and consumption of polite literature and other forms of leisure associated with the cultural refinements of the leisured classes (see Plumb and McKendrick). The taste for politeness helped to spread a set of assumptions and values that created a unified national bourgeoisie. In the British cultural provinces, the desire to be accepted into this polite society led to the constitution of college English studies. Such initiatives often become evident on the borders of the established hegemony, for those who would map the boundaries of acceptable usage must concentrate their efforts there, and those seeking admission to the dominant discourse will have to pass through its margins.

Gramsci would encourage us to ask who these intellectuals spoke for, what groups their theories authorized, and how their articulation of shared experiences and objectives strengthened or challenged the established hegemony. One could easily reduce these figures to mere reactionaries. Like traditional intellectuals then and now, the first teachers of college English claimed that their universalized concepts of culture and language were free of factional self-interests. Despite claims to be disinterested observers, such figures as Blair and Campbell clearly spoke for the cultural hegemony of the British middle classes and the political authority of the Whig establishment. One could easily use such judgments to dismiss these figures and ignore the complexity of the historical context. On the other hand, one could argue that the first teachers of English were actually organic intellectuals of the progressive bourgeoisie. They did help to improve economic conditions, ease restrictions on religious and personal freedoms, and foster critical literacy in the vernacular at a time when traditional intellectuals in English universities were still preserving a dead language that could only serve the needs of the gentry and their clerics. While Blair and Campbell preached political quietism on days that the government set aside for reflection on the revolutions in France and America, they also preached tolerance and freedom of inquiry at a time when Catholics were denied basic rights and skeptics like Hume were seen as heretics who needed to be publicly punished.

To fit such figures into a unified, univocal rhetorical tradition, we are tempted to simplify them and the contexts to which they responded. On one hand, they were progressive intellectuals who translated the humanities into the contemporary cultural idiom to make them relevant to a broader public. On the other hand, they followed traditional intellectuals in identifying that public as a "republic of letters" that stood above class interests and political conflicts.

Like traditional intellectuals then and now, the first teachers of college English saw themselves as "men of letters" who were disinterested observers of public conflicts. English was thus taught as a means of personal self-improvement and a class marker to distinguish the politely educated from those beneath them in the social hierarchy. Like the first teachers of English, traditional intellectuals have generally failed to become deeply engaged with social change because they have identified themselves with broader ties to like-minded intellectuals rather than establishing deeper contacts with social groups beneath the cultural elite.

To provide an example of how traditional intellectuals generally fail to become engaged with popular social movements, Gramsci contrasts the Reformation's effect on all of society with the Renaissance of intellectual culture (*Prison Notebooks* 132n). Valuing the Reformation over the Renaissance may be disconcerting to us because we tend to write the Reformation out of our history and make the Renaissance a central transition in the rhetorical tradition. Gramsci would of course challenge our whole sense of tradition. He would ask why we limit our past to a scattered group of intellectuals and why we have dislocated them from their social contexts. He would suggest that we should be studying history to learn how to speak to changing social practices, at least that is what we need to be doing if we want to be more than traditional intellectuals.

The rhetorical tradition is a fiction that has outlasted its usefulness because we need to be using history to pursue deeper inquiries into the dialectical relationship of intellectual and social change. We have given up the idea that intellectual history is merely the history of intellectuals; perhaps the time has come to quit confining the history of rhetoric to theories of composition. An historical perspective more concerned with social change can make important contributions to research and teaching. For example, localized historical studies are directly consistent with the work of Paulo Freire, who has encouraged us to study and teach the "nuclei of contradiction" that define the experience of specific discourse communities (104). These unresolved contradictions are the rhetorical situations that we must study if we want to understand how communities put shared beliefs into social practice.

Historical inquiries into the contradictions and continuities of broader historical formations can also help us to expand our sense of the current field of study. The borders of rhetoric and composition are no longer set by the turf fights with literary scholars that established the field. We have formed broader alliances and interests, and the conflicts that define us have now shifted to the unmapped borders between cultural studies and rhetoric and composition. We need to develop a broader scope and new methods of inquiry that can help us to speak to these developments, and through them to the social changes that are reconstituting the humanities to include the traditions of more diverse social groups.

Notes

1. There has been little debate of the canon in particular or historical methods in general (see Jarratt, Schilb, Berlin, Connors, and especially Vitanza, who promises a book on the topic).

2. While one would not want to ignore the well-known work of Berlin and Connors, the lack of historical research on college English is evident in the fact that a forty-year-old dissertation (recently reprinted by Southern Methodist UP) is still an authoritative source on the nineteenth century, and the best studies of early American rhetoric are speech articles that are equally as old (see Kitzhaber and Guthrie). Horner's bibliographies have done much to encourage the needed research.

3. *The New Cultural History* (1989) edited by Lynn Hunt provides a good sample of this research, which draws on Foucault and Geertz as well as Bakhtin. The work of Shirley Brice Heath is of course the classic example of this sort of work within our established field of study.

4. *The History of Women; Guide to Microfilms Collections* (1983) is another essential source for those interested in reinventing the rhetorical traditions of women (see also Frei, Frei, and Schneider; Hinding and Chambers).

5. Moore wrote over fifty of the popular tales and ballads in the series of Cheap Repository Tracts that was intended to supplant Paine's irreligious and seditious influence. The Tracts were designed to look like chapbooks with flashy titles and bold woodcuts. In just six weeks in 1795, 300,000 copies were sold, and a better printing was made for the children of the gentry. According to Altick, "Tom Paine and Hannah Moore between them had opened the book to the common English reader" (77).

Works Cited

Adamson, Walter L. *Hegemony and Revolution: A Study of Antonio Gramsci's Political and Cultural Theory.* Berkeley: U of California P, 1980.

Altick, Richard D. *The English Common Reader: A Social History of the Mass Reading Public.* Chicago: U of Chicago P, 1957.

Bakhtin, Mikhail. *Dialogic Imagination.* Ed. Michael Holquist. Austin: U of Texas P, 1981.

Berlin, James. "Revisionary History: The Dialectical Method." *PRE/TEXT* 8 (1987): 47–61.

Connors, Robert J. "Historical Inquiry in Composition Studies." *The Writing Instructor* 4 (1984): 157–67.

Eagleton, Terry. *The Function of Criticism from the Spectator to Poststructuralism.* London: Verso, 1984.

Evans, Charles. *American Bibliography: A Chronological Dictionary of All Books, Pamphlets and Periodicals Printed in the United States . . . to . . . 1820.* 14 vols. New York: Peter Smith, 1941.

Frei, Linda, Marcia Frei, and Joanne Schneider, eds. *Women in Western European History: A Select Chronological, Geographical and Topical Bibliography from Antiquity to the French Revolution.* Westport, CT: Greenwood, 1982.

Freire, Paulo. *Pedagogy of the Oppressed.* New York: Continuum, 1970.

Geertz, Clifford. *The Interpretation of Cultures.* New York: Basic, 1973.

Graff, Harvey J. *The Legacies of Literacy.* Bloomington: Indiana UP, 1987.

Gramsci, Antonio. *Selections from Cultural Writings.* Ed. David Forgacs and Geoffrey Nowell-Smith. Trans. William Boelhower. London: Lawrence and Wishart, 1985.

———. *Selections from the Prison Notebooks.* Ed. and Trans. Quentin Hoare and Geoffrey Nowell Smith. New York: International, 1971.

Guthrie, Warren. "The Development of Rhetorical Theory in America, 1635–1800." *Speech Monographs* 13–15 (1946–48): 14–22, 38–54, 61–71.

Heath, Shirley Brice. *Ways with Words.* Cambridge: Cambridge UP, 1983.

Hinding, Andrea, and Clark Chambers, eds. *Women's History Sources: A Guide to Archives and Manuscript Collections in the U.S.* New York: Bowker, 1979.

History of Women: Guide to Microfilm Collections. Woodbridge, CT: Research Publications, 1983.

Horner, Winifred Bryan. "Nineteenth-Century Rhetoric at the Universities of Aberdeen and St. Andrews with an Annotated Bibliography of Archival Materials." *Rhetoric Society Quarterly* 20 (Summer 1990): 287–99.

————. "Nineteenth-Century Rhetoric at the University of Edinburgh with an Annotated Bibliography of Archival Materials." *Rhetoric Society Quarterly* 19 (Fall 1989): 365–75.

————. "Nineteenth-Century Rhetoric at the University of Glasgow with an Annotated Bibliography of Archival Materials." *Rhetoric Society Quarterly* 20 (Spring 1990): 173–85.

————. *The Present State of Scholarship in Historical and Contemporary Rhetoric.* Rev. ed. Columbia: U of Missouri P, 1990.

Hunt, Lynn, ed. *The New Cultural History.* Berkeley: U of California P, 1989.

Jarratt, Susan C. "Toward a Sophistic Historiography." *PRE/TEXT* 8 (1987): 9–26.

Kerber, Linda K. *Women of the Republic: Intellect and Ideology in Revolutionary America.* Chapel Hill: U of North Carolina P, 1980.

Kitzhaber, Albert Raymond. "Rhetoric in American Colleges, 1850–1900." PhD Diss. University of Washington, 1953. Rpt. Southern Methodist UP, 1990.

Lacquer, Thomas. "The Cultural Origins of Popular Literacy in England 1500–1850." *Oxford Review of Education* 2 (1976): 255–75.

McKendrick, Neil. "The Consumer Revolution of Eighteenth-Century England." *The Birth of a Consumer Society.* London: Europa, 1982. 9–33.

Miller, Thomas P. "The Formation of College English: A Survey of the Archives of Eighteenth-Century Rhetorical Theory and Practice." *Rhetoric Society Quarterly* 20 (1990): 261–86.

————. "Where Did College English Studies Come From?" *Rhetoric Review* 9 (1990): 50–69.

Plumb, J. H. "The Commercialization of Leisure in Eighteenth-Century England." *The Birth of a Consumer Society.* London: Europa, 1982. 265–85.

Salamini, Leonardo. *The Sociology of Political Praxis: An Introduction to Gramsci's Theory.* London: Routledge, 1981.

Schilb, John. "The History of Rhetoric and the Rhetoric of History." *PRE/TEXT* 7 (1986): 11–34.

Thompson, E. P. *The Making of the English Working Classes.* New York: Vintage, 1966.

Turner, William. *The Warrington Academy Monthly Repository.* 8–10 (1813–15). Rpt. NP: Warrington Library and Museum Comm., 1957.

Vitanza, Victor J. " 'Notes' Towards Historiographies of Rhetorics; or the Rhetorics of the Histories of Rhetorics: Traditional, Revisionary, and Sub/Versive." *PRE/TEXT* 8 (1987): 63–125.

Watt, Ian. *The Rise of the Novel.* Berkeley: U of California P, 1965.

4

A Model for Our Time
Fred Newton Scott's Rhetoric
Program at Michigan

Donald C. Stewart

In the nineteenth-century background material they supply for *The Rhetorical Tradition,* Patricia Bizzell and Bruce Herzberg have but two observations on the work of Fred Newton Scott of Michigan. Drawing on James Berlin's *Writing Instruction in Nineteenth-Century American Colleges,* they describe briefly the "stripped-down" rhetoric that emerged late in the century, a rhetoric heavily influenced by Alexander Bain and A. S. Hill and then note that "the efforts of teachers like Fred Newton Scott and a few others to criticize such methods and improve this gloomy situation produced no competing rhetorical theory or pedagogy" (664–65). They qualify this remark by observing, in addition, that "only recently have scholars begun to examine Scott's insistence on the value of the rhetorical tradition in composition teaching, his use of linguistics and behavioral psychology, his emphasis on the composing process, and his sensitivity to the social uses of language" (665). Two hundred pages later they cite Scott's "English Composition as Mode of Behavior," published in 1922, and observe that "aside from encouraging teachers to exercise greater sympathy, Scott offers no new rhetoric that will point another way" (862–63).

These are really quite astonishing generalizations because they do not begin to do justice to the work Berlin, Albert Kitzhaber, and I have published about Scott and, more than anything else, reveal a stunning ignorance of Scott's rhetoric program at Michigan.

Berlin's analysis of Scott's work—quite good in many respects—is flawed by his desire to establish Emerson and Dewey as major influences on Scott's intellectual development and to identify him as an early social constructionist in his thinking about rhetoric. We now know that at least part of Scott's intellectual roots are in German transcendental philosophy, to which he was introduced by William Jones, first president of Indiana State University, when Scott was a student in the university's lab schools. Jones also introduced him—both directly and through the training he gave the staff that taught Scott and his fellow students—to habits of intellectual inquiry that characterized Scott's thinking all his life.

Scott himself would probably have been quite surprised at the notion that John Dewey was an influence on him. The two men were actually close friends and associates, both during the years they were at Michigan and later. Although hard evidence is lacking, there is ample suggestion in Scott's informal biographical sketch of Dewey, which he wrote in 1891 for *The Castalian,* a campus publication, and in a number of his diary entries, that the two men exerted mutual influence on each other's thinking.

Berlin is on much safer ground identifying Scott as an early social constructionist because one repeatedly finds in Scott's work his insistence on rhetoric in a social context. Whether or not he would have been willing to accept the notion that reality is as much constructed by language as modern social constructionists assert is another matter. The important point, which Berlin makes quite emphatically, is that Scott was shaping an alternative to the dominant current-traditional rhetoric of the time. The failure to utilize it lay not with Scott but with composition teachers of the era who either were ignorant of the alternative he did offer or knew about it and still did not take advantage of it.

Kitzhaber's assessment of Scott's work is more comprehensive and balanced than Berlin's. He refers to specific courses in Michigan's rhetoric program and is aware of the diversity of Scott's interests, not only in rhetorical history, theory, and practice but in aesthetics and journalism. Kitzhaber is also alert to the interdisciplinary nature of Scott's program. "Scott . . . made a genuine effort to formulate a comprehensive system of rhetorical theory drawing on new developments in such related disciplines as experimental psychology, linguistics, and sociology" (69).

Apparently, the fact that such observations point clearly to a well-established and comprehensive rhetoric program and that this program offered a distinct alternative to the widely imitated but impoverished model Harvard provided simply did not register with Bizzell and Herzberg. I think it time, therefore, to enlighten them and others who are equally uninformed about what was happening in Ann Arbor nearly a century ago.

The best terms to describe Scott's program are either *catholic* or *comprehensive* because these best characterize the mind of the man who established it. "Dr. Scott's conception of rhetoric was catholic in the extreme; it was limited only by the range of his own personal interests, which really means that it was not limited at all" (Strauss 332).

Scott had made this abundantly clear in the entry on rhetoric which he had prepared for Dodd & Mead's *International Encyclopedia* in 1903. He defines it as follows:

> Taken broadly, the science and art of communication in language. . . . [r]egarded from the scientific point of view, rhetoric properly belongs to that branch of knowledge which is concerned with the relations of men in society. In every community a great variety of activities go on simultaneously. One important group of these activities consists of all the processes by which men express themselves and convey their thoughts and feelings to their fellows. It includes not only the more primitive modes of thought conveyance, such as gesture, picture writing, and the like, but also the most highly elaborated modes, such as the arts of architecture, sculpture, music, painting, and oral and written speech. This large class may be subdivided in two ways: (1) according to the medium employed in the process of thought conveyance, and (2) accordingly as the emphasis is thrown upon the individual or the social phase of the process. The first method of classification leads to the differentiation of the several arts; the second to the distinction of processes mainly self-expressive from processes mainly communicative. The subject matter of rhetoric is thus seen to be distinguished from that of allied sciences by the fact (1) that its medium is language and (2) that the emphasis is thrown upon the phase of communication, i.e., upon prose. But although rhetoric is primarily the science of

communication, it is still concerned to a large extent with questions of expression. (763)

Two points are worth making about this definition of rhetoric. First, one notes the orderly way in which Scott places the subject in the context of related human activities. Second, while he asserts that rhetoric is primarily the science of communication and thus plays a key role in social processes, thus appearing to take a position congenial to modern social constructionists, he tempers that observation by recognizing that rhetoric is also much concerned with problems of expression, by which he means the individual's efforts to find his or her own intellectual center and voice.

He then continues his discussion of rhetoric by saying that "the underlying problem of rhetoric concerns the reciprocal speech relations of the individual and the community" (763) and then identifying the three principal phases of the problem.

I. *Psychological problems* relating (1) to the nature of the writing or speaking man, (2) to the mental activities involved in the process of composing. Here arise questions regarding (a) the nature and genesis of expression, (b) the characteristics of genius, (c) the acquirement and cultivation of the speech habit, and (d) the factors operating in the experience of the individual to turn his self-expression into the communicative channel. . . .

II. *Social problems,* relating to the dynamic effect of speech upon the community of hearers or readers. The assumption which underlies discussion of the subject from this point of view is that language is preëminently the social bond. The main questions relate (1) to the typical modes of response on the part of individuals and groups of individuals in the community, (2) to the formation of social or public opinion. . . .

III. *Formal problems,* relating to the medium of communication, viz., language in organized form. The main problems concern (1) the nature and origin of discourse; (2) the peculiar function of discourse, as (a) on one side the expression of the individual and (b) on the other the means of social interchange; (3) the structure or morphology of discourse in (a) its minuter forms (words, sentences, paragraphs, etc.), (b) its larger forms (whole composition), (c) its typical modes (description, narration, exposition, etc.); and (4) the typical methods of distribution (books, newspapers, etc.). (763–64)

Scott notes that the formal aspect of rhetoric has been treated in considerable detail in both ancient and modern treatises on rhetoric but that it has not been "consistently unified or properly connected with the other two phases" (764).

He says further that the principle of organic unity is the most fundamental yet developed to explain rhetoric's structural side, "and from it may be derived all of the usual rhetorical qualities" (764). And then—in a passage which would greatly please today's social constructionists, transactionalists, and epistemic rhetoricians—he observes that

> [T]he truth is that all such principles are derivative, not primary. A truly scientific exposition would demonstrate that the peculiar forms and qualities of any piece of discourse are the natural outcome of the interaction of the individual and society in the process of communication. An oration, e.g., is the product of two forces, (1) the impulse of the individual to a certain kind of self-expression, and (2) the demand of the social mind for a certain kind of communication. The oration is the meeting point of these two forces. (764)   *literature*

In 1903 Michigan's English department was divided and Scott's rhetoric department was born. In earlier papers on Scott, I have speculated that this division might have been accompanied by some friction between members of the divided departments, particularly between Isaac Demmon, the veteran English department head and Scott, who might have been perceived as an ambitious upstart. The Regents' Minutes, both published and unpublished, indicate otherwise. Demmon recommended the division because of the distinction with which Scott had conducted the work in rhetoric for more than a decade, and the two men, as Scott's diary reveals, remained on cordial terms the rest of their lives. Demmon never threatened Scott's rhetoric program, but the same cannot be said of his successors who exerted considerable energy in the 1920s to bring about the demise of the rhetoric department and its absorption into the English department.

social criterion like

One could pick any number of years as exemplifying the scope and depth of the program Scott developed, but I choose 1910 because by then adjustments had been made in staff and courses and the program had taken the shape that characterized it for much of the rest of its existence. The calendar for that year notes that the department offered four different kinds of courses:

> (1) Courses intended primarily to give the student practice in the leading types of prose composition. These include Courses 1, 2, 3, 4, 15, and 20. (2) Courses intended primarily to familiarize the student with the fundamental principles of rhetoric and criticism. These include courses 5, 7, 8, 9, 10, 12, 16, and 17. Courses 7, 8, 12, 23, and 24 combine advanced composition with the study of rhetoric and critical theory. (3) Course 6, designed primarily for students who intend to teach. (4) Courses for students who are preparing for newspaper work. (Calendar 1910–11: 128)

Courses 1 and 2, clearly the equivalent of modern freshman composition courses, are called "Composition and Rhetoric," are described in the calendar as introductory, and "aim to promote clearness and correctness of expression through practice in the simpler kinds of composition" (128). Nineteen sections were provided for in the fall of 1910, and these were taught by Scott's staff, some of whom had recently acquired MA or PhD degrees and some of whom were still working toward them.

Courses 3 and 4, "Advanced Composition and Rhetoric," intended for second year students, were organized around the popular Forms or Modes of Discourse, Narration and Description in course 3 and Exposition and Argument in course 4. Their purpose was to offer students "systematic practice in the four principal types of prose composition" (128).

To this point one finds nothing especially innovative or exemplary in Scott's program. The reasons are quite obvious. These four courses, plus 15, which was a course in argumentative writing, are essentially practical rhetoric, directed at students who have neither the interest nor the ability to deal with more abstract theoretical and technical issues in composition. They were the kinds of courses for which Scott and Denney wrote their textbooks: *Paragraph Writing, Composition-Rhetoric, Elementary English Composition,* and *Composition-Literature.* However, as Berlin notes, even at this level, Scott's approach to rhetoric differed from that of most of his contemporaries. He never let his students forget that writing existed in a social context, that the work of the classroom was not a hothouse plant, serving a purpose only in that place and having no bearing on real life and language.

A year earlier, in "What the West Wants in Preparatory Education," Scott had made this point emphatically, implicitly scolding both the attitude of the Harvard examiners and teachers of composition who promoted the priorities of current-traditional rhetoric:

> It is of course necessary that our young people should spell and punctuate properly, should make the verb agree with its subject, should use words in their dictionary senses and write sentences that can be read aloud without causing unnecessary pain to the mandibles. They should also know the meanings of the words in the poetry and prose that they read, and understand the allusions to things ancient and modern. But these matters after all, are subsidiary and must be treated as such. They are means to an end. To treat them as an end in and for themselves is to turn education in this subject upside down. The main purpose of training in composition is free speech, direct and sincere communion with our fellows, that swift and untrammeled exchange of opinion, feeling, and experience, which is the working instrument of the social instinct and the motive power of civilization. The teacher of composition who does not somehow make his pupils realize this and feel that all of the verbal machinery is but for the purpose of fulfilling this great end, is false to his trust. (17–19)

The one course that may seem a bit out of place among the five cited is Thomas Rankin's course 20, a class in short story writing. It seems out of place to us today because of the split that has occurred between expository and creative writing since the end of World War II. To Scott, however, that division would have been illogical. Prose composition included anything that was not clearly poetry. And it is significant that his program reflects that perception even at its most practical level.

The second group of courses identified by the calendar formed the core of the truly original work that took place in Scott's department. Their purpose, we recall, was "to familiarize the student with the fundamental principles of Rhetoric and Criticism" (128). How thoroughly they did that, for students who applied themselves, will quickly become apparent. Two of the courses, 5 and 16, focused primarily on style. The description for course 5 says simply that it "is intended to meet the needs of the student in two respects: namely, to open the way to the study of criticism through practice in observing the details of literary workmanship, and to afford such a concrete and practical view of the principles of good writing as may help the student to better his own expression" (130).

One gets a more detailed picture of how those goals were met from a pamphlet Scott published twenty years earlier, "The Principles of Style." It is essentially a bibliography with a prefatory essay. In the latter, Scott says specifically that he had prepared it for students taking a class in the principles of style. To acquaint readers with the purpose of the course, he differentiated between students who never progressed beyond a practical understanding of strategies for writing and those who began to extract from concrete operations some larger abstract principles. The latter are still one stage below those, however, who progress from an understanding of the science of rhetoric to an appreciation of what Scott calls the "higher rhetoric," which is characterized by refinement of taste and a sense of the development of the writer's authentic voice:

> The student's practice—his paragraphing, the management of the rhythm of his prose, even his capitalizing, spelling and punctuation—ought to come more easily and naturally to him through this infusion of life into dry bones. And as for the grasp of principles, he will probably come to wonder whether, before, he ever had hold of any principles at all, so vividly does he now realize for the first time that whatever is not a piece of his own personality can be nothing but . . . a paste-board box to hold abstractions.
>
> A piece of his own personality!—that, after all, is, in the higher rhetoric, the only kind of goods worth having. (7)

The purpose of the course, then, was to help students toward a better understanding of the higher rhetoric. The work of the course included (1) lectures "designed to relate the familiar rules of the Lower Rhetoric to some of the primary facts of Logic, Psychology and Aesthetics, and to lay a more philosophical foundation for the student's own investigations" (9); (2) the students' own research in which they examined essays in criticism "to discover upon what basis famous critics have founded their judgments of literature," "reading of treatises on style," and essays on special topics chosen by each; and (3) study of specimens of style to verify principles. For the latter Scott was using, in 1890, Saintsbury's *Specimens of English Prose* or Genung's *Handbook of Rhetorical Analysis*. What he may have been using twenty years later is not known.

The bibliography itself groups more than a hundred items under the following headings: "Definition and Classification of Literature"; "Relations of Thought and Language"; "Poetry and Prose"; "Rhythm and Meter"; "Tone, Color and Harmony"; "Figures"; "The Logical Structure"; and "Definition of Style." In addition, he supplies a list of treatises on style, rhetorics, and topics for personal research, both technical and advanced. The authors and works that appear in these lists extend from classical times (Aristotle's *Rhetoric,* for example) to work by contemporaries (Pater and Saintsbury). There are, in addition, brief descriptive notes on some of the works.

Most astonishing is Scott's observation, in his preface, that these "lists are intended to be suggestive merely, and in consequence, no high degree of comprehensiveness has been aimed at" (11). That is either an excessively modest observation or, more likely, a true indication of the thoroughness with which Scott did all of his work. There is no doubt at all that any student taking this course would leave it with a deep and comprehensive sense of issues involving style.

Course 16, "Modern English Prose," is described as a

> course in the development of English prose style. The various styles of writing prose which are characteristic of the successive periods of modern English literature will be taken up in order.

Special attention will be given to the relations between changes in literary style and general changes in the social life of the nation. The works studied will choose in the main from the writings of the following authors: Sidney, Lyly, Bacon, Milton, Dryden, Addison, Johnson, Lamb, Carlyle, Macauley, Arnold, and Stevenson. (132)

This was John Brumm's course, and its focus seems to have been slightly different from Scott's, but there is no doubt that it was a substantial offering on the subject of style.

This block also includes course 12, the writing of reviews; course 17, diction and usage; and course 8, the study and writing of short stories. The inclusion of review and short story writing in the same general group again demonstrates the latitude of Scott's perception of the province of rhetoric, his refusal to separate creative from more practical expository writing. We do not know exactly how Scott conducted course 8, but a reading list for it is included in his papers. One finds twenty-six titles on the list, among them Dickens's *Tale of Two Cities* and *Edwin Drood,* George Eliot's *Mill on the Floss,* Thackeray's *Vanity Fair,* Meredith's *Egoist,* and Melville's *Moby Dick.* Considering the length of some of these books and the size of the list, one wonders whether, indeed, students did read all of them or were expected to have read a good many before taking the course. Since it was open only to those who received special permission, Scott no doubt limited it to students he knew had read or were capable of reading the material.

In 1908 he introduced course 23, "Seminary in Advanced Composition," which was also a year's course, becoming 24 in the spring semester. It was "intended for a limited number of advanced students who write with facility and are in the habit of writing, but who desire personal criticism and direction. Although the greater part of the time will be spent in the discussion of the manuscripts submitted for correction, there will be talks upon the essentials of English Composition and the principles of criticism and revision" (131). It was open only to students who received special permission.

Of this course Clarence Thorpe wrote in the article on the rhetoric department for the Michigan encyclopedia:

This was destined to become one of the most prized offerings of the department. Since only a limited number could be accommodated and since only candidates of ability were selected, it soon came to be regarded as an honor to be admitted to the course. The class became something like a young writers' club, and was a proving ground for many who later gained distinction in the literary field. It was, moreover, a recognition, in principle, of the importance of creative writing as a university study. To it, more than to anything else, can be traced the Hopwood prizes and the outstanding development of present advanced courses in writing at the University of Michigan. (563)

The course in diction and usage, we may infer, was the department's opportunity to espouse a descriptive rather than a prescriptive approach to the subject of English usage. It was no accident that Sterling Leonard, Ruth Weeks, and Charles Fries, individuals who championed more liberal attitudes toward this subject, were all Scott students and may have taken this course or one similar to it.

Course 7, "Interpretations of Literature and Art," provided yet another dimension to this block of courses. The catalog says that "the first weeks of the course are given to a discussion of critical principles. These principles are then applied in the appreciation and interpretation of specimens of literature and art" (130). It was open only to seniors and graduates and was conducted as a seminar. Scott's interest in aesthetics had begun early in his career and continued unabated. We know this because John Dewey, when he assumed the headship of the philosophy department at Michigan in 1889, the year of Scott's first appointment, had specifically requested that Scott be available to teach an aesthetics course in that department, and Scott had done that for several years. When Dewey left, Scott continued to offer the aesthetics course, which became course 7 in the rhetoric department's program.

In 1890 Scott had also published a brochure entitled "Aesthetics, Its Problems and Literature" a pamphlet elaborately praised by William Torrey Harris, then U.S. Commissioner of Education. Nine years later he collaborated with his former teacher and good friend, Charles Mills Gayley, in *An Introduc-*

tion to the Methods and Materials of Literary Criticism: The Bases in Aesthetics and Poetics, a very substantial work of some 587 pages. Under five major headings, "Nature and Function of Literary Criticism," "Principles of Art," "Principles of Literature," "The Theory of Poetry," and "The Principles of Versification," it contains definitions, notes both on general subjects and particular authors, and extensive bibliographies.

The central course in this block, however, was course 9, the seminar in rhetoric and criticism. Actually, it was a full year's course, 9 in the fall and 10 in the spring semesters, and is described as follows. "The subjects of discussion vary from year to year. Among the problems to be investigated are the following: The origins of prose; the nature and origin of the leading types of discourse; the psychology of figures of speech; the rhythm of prose; the sociological basis of the principles of usage; the origin, development, and laws of the process of communication" (130). In short, everything that Scott had defined in the encyclopedia entry as the province of rhetoric, was eventually taken up in this course. It was open only to graduate students, but it exemplifies the kind of work Scott was doing that made graduate study in the department so attractive.

> Graduate study in rhetoric was characterized throughout the existence of the department not only by a broadly liberal point of view in linguistics, with a consistent emphasis upon the growth of language as a social phenomenon and as an instrument for current needs, but also by critical attitudes which had their bases in psychological investigation and in an examination of literature in its relation to life. Merely historical matters were subordinated to the analysis of works and to an understanding of the principles by which their authors write and of the sources and modes of their appeal. Scott's own deep humanism permeated the work of the entire department, and graduate study in rhetoric became synonymous with an earnest search for central standards in artistic creation and aesthetic response. (Thorpe 562)

Clearly, the work of this course, all graduate work in rhetoric in Scott's department, anticipates modern rhetoricians' interests in the relationships between rhetoric and linguistics, sociology, anthropology, psychology, and related fields by nearly one hundred years. Small wonder that Scott resented the implication that Harvard was a source of ideas for the teaching of composition when its program offered nothing more than a series of practical writing courses and a graduate course in classroom management and paper grading. Scott's program would be judged extremely sophisticated and intellectually rigorous by modern standards.

There were also, as noted earlier, two other dimensions to the work of Scott's department: pedagogy and journalism. Course 6 (originally English 17), a seminar in methods of teaching English composition and rhetoric, drew fifty students the first year Scott offered it, 1897, and it continued to be a popular course in the rhetoric department. One can assume quite safely that philosophically and theoretically it reflected the emphases we have seen in other phases of the rhetoric department's program and offered, in addition, practical assistance in the teacher's daily classroom work.

As early as 1891, Scott had offered a journalism course, "Rapid Writing," believed to be only the second in actual newspaper writing offered in the country. (Missouri's David Russell McAnally had offered the first in 1879.) By 1910 Scott's rhetoric department offered several journalism courses: 13, 14, 25, and 26. Course 13, "The Newspaper: Its Nature, Function, and Development" was "intended for students who are preparing to do newspaper work" (130). It was conducted as a seminar and students had to get special permission to enroll in it. Course 14 offered practice in writing news stories, feature articles, interviews, correspondence, and editorials. Courses 25 and 26 are simply described as "practical newspaper work."

Scott's purpose in offering journalism courses derived from his broad conception of rhetoric. He saw the newspaper as the means for distributing intelligence throughout the community and thus was concerned that those responsible for producing it were philosophically and intellectually responsible. One might say that he saw it as a kind of public rhetoric. Although writers of the biographical sketches that appeared shortly after Scott's death in 1931 were unaware of the fact, in 1886 and 1887 he had worked for two small papers in Cleveland, and he never lost interest in all facets of newspaper work, from gathering of material to the actual production of papers.

In 1905 through 1908, Scott collaborated with two of his staff members in offering courses 15 and 16, "Reporting and Editorial Work," again full-year courses, the lower number being assigned to the fall semester. Notably, he did not miss an opportunity to acquire materials for his journalism classes. The 10 October 1905 Regents' Minutes report that Professor Scott asked for fifteen dollars to acquire the manuscript, proofs, and sketches used in producing the Sunday, 1 October edition of the *Chicago Record-Herald*. In his memo to the Regents, Scott notes that the collection includes

> 1. All of the manuscript prepared by the editors, reporters and other members of the staff. It includes both the manuscripts which were used and those which, for one reason or another, were unused. These corrected and unused manuscripts are especially interesting as showing the methods of copy-reading and editing employed in the office of a large newspaper.
> 2. The originals of the cartoons and other illustrative matter.
> 3. A number of "matts" showing the method of stereotyping the forms.
> 4. A complete set of proofs and revises, with the alterations and corrections made by the proofreaders.
> 5. Copies of the various editions of the paper of the date mentioned.

Scott concludes by observing that "the collection is of considerable educative value for students who are fitting themselves for newspaper work, since it shows in a striking way the characteristic features of modern newspaper procedure" (633–34).

Course 25, which first appears in the Michigan calendar in the fall of 1910, is a bit of a puzzle. For reasons Scott never makes clear in his diary, getting it approved was a worry to him. Entries in the months previous to the announcement of this course refer to his working up the course announcement and imply that he was getting some resistance from faculty in the literary department. One can only speculate that the resistance came from those who would see in work of this kind considerably less intellectual rigor than that required by traditional courses offered by the department.

Course numbers and descriptions do not give a complete picture of an academic program or the way in which it is presented by the individuals who have shaped it. It is appropriate therefore, to take a closer look at the testimony of two of Scott's students, testimony that gives us a revealing picture of Scott in the classroom and indicates why he was so revered by many of them.

In a collection of reminiscences to which several individuals contributed a few years after Scott's death is a brief but fine paper from Shirley Smith titled "Fred Newton Scott as a Teacher."[1] He describes Scott's classroom manner as "effortless," "(he did everything as he polished his eyeglasses, gently)" and conjectures that it "had been consciously cultivated to save nervous energy, to avoid the distraction of noise or motion" (12). Apparently, Scott conducted classes in a voice sufficiently subdued that Smith was astonished the first time he heard him deliver a public lecture. "I would not have believed till then that he had a voice that could fill so great a space" (12).

He described Scott's teaching technique as Socratic and noted that he was a master of it. Looking back, his students had difficulty saying just what Scott was an authority on or what he had said to them specifically. He exerted tremendous energy, says Smith, probing, cross-examining, and interrogating members of his classes, leading them to the critical insights he wished them to discover. "The things that shaped us in his classes were thoughts that developed there in us or others, and whether or to what extent they came from Scott, we couldn't say. He made us possess ourselves of more than judgments; he made us acquire criteria; he made us develop our own resources of taste, appreciation; he taught us to appraise, and helped us to find standards of value" (13).

Smith notes that unlike his contemporaries, Scott did not consider editorial conventions—spelling, punctuation, and usage—to be of paramount concern in writing. He attended to these matters, of course, but Smith says the emphasis in Scott's classes was always on the use to which words were being put, in essence their appropriateness and precision in the many contexts in which they appeared. And he recalls one of Scott's favorite teaching devices: presenting students with a variety of passages from which important adjectives, nouns, or verbs had been omitted, with accompanying lists of words that could be used in the blanks. "It was astonishing until we got used to these discussions how heated even a football guard or a prospective chemist who had elected the course wrathfully, because it was required work, could get over such questions as whether an ice-coated branch glittered or glistened or glowed in the winter sunshine, or what noun would best convey the succession of sounds of blows exchanged by mailed knights in mortal sword combat" (14). Scott employed many such devices, and it is a pity that Smith did not describe more of them.

Smith concludes with a remarkable tribute to Scott the teacher.

> He had the capacity—and he exercised it as naturally as he breathed—to keep alive in any student any enthusiasm for beauty or depth in literature that the student was lucky enough to have. He could at the same time sharpen the critical judgment, widen the range of interests, and demand the intellectual honesty that is the best sort of discipline. None could surpass him in ability to communicate a sense of distinction in aesthetic enjoyment, together with a wide and open-minded catholicity of taste. And to most of us, finally, his immense mental energy was one of our first and most enduring lessons in the means by which great things are achieved. (15)

That this was so is demonstrated abundantly by Ray Stannard Baker, who in 1928 recalled his experience in Scott's classroom and said of it:

> I have always felt that Prof. Scott gave me more than any other teacher at Michigan or elsewhere. I took his courses at a time when I was confused in my own mind as to my own capacity as to what I could best devote myself to. I found in the two courses

with Prof. Scott, which I deserted the law school to take, the liberation which I was seeking. He seemed to have the rare gift of setting men to thinking and then, by deft touches of advice—not too much of it—indicating the reading which would best enlarge the vista. As a result, I deserted the law course which I was supposed to be taking and spent all my time at the library developing themes which were suggested by discussions in Prof. Scott's seminars. I am sure he never knew the number of books I read nor the darkness of intelligence applied to some of them. I think, also, if it had not been for Prof. Scott, I should have graduated with the perfectly innocuous degree of Bachelor of Law from the University of Michigan; but he made me so hot to begin actual practice of the calling to which he inspired me, that I deserted the University, having learned how to educate myself, and never got the degree, which was one of the happiest incidents of my life.

This then is the man, and this the program, that offered such rich alternatives to Harvard's current-traditional approach to the teaching of rhetoric and composition in the late nineteenth and early twentieth centuries. Can anyone question now our reasons for lamenting the fact that too many English teachers of that era turned to Cambridge, not to Ann Arbor, for direction in this subject? And can anyone wonder at our astonishment at the observation that Scott offered no alternative to the current-traditional paradigm that became dominant at that time?

Note

1. Others who contributed were Professor Richard R. Kirk of Tulane; Professor Karl Young of Yale; Lyman J. Bryson, director of the California Association for Adult Education; S. Emory Thomason, publisher of the *Chicago Daily Times;* Lee A. White of the *Detroit News;* and Arthur Pound, author, of New Scotland, New York.

Works Cited

Baker, Ray Stannard. Letter to Willard Thorpe. 20 December 1928.
    Fred Newton Scott Papers. Michigan Historical Collections. Ann
    Arbor, Michigan.

Berlin, James A. *Writing Instruction in Nineteenth-Century American
    Colleges.* Carbondale: Southern Illinois UP, 1984.

Bizzell, Patricia, and Bruce Herzberg, eds. *The Rhetorical Tradition: Readings from Classical Times to the Present.* New York: St. Martin's, 1990.

Gayley, Charles Mills, and Fred Newton Scott. *An Introduction to the Methods and Materials of Literary Criticism.* Boston, 1899.

Genung, John. *Handbook of Rhetorical Analysis.* Boston, 1889.

Kitzhaber, Albert R. *Rhetoric in American Colleges: 1850–1900.* Diss. U. of Washington, 1953. Dallas: Southern Methodist UP, 1990.

Saintsbury, George. *Specimens of English Prose.* 1885.

Scott, Fred Newton. *Aesthetics: Its Problems and Literature.* Ann Arbor: U of Michigan, 1890.

_____. "John Dewey." *Castalian* (1891): 23–29.

_____. *The Principles of Style.* Ann Arbor: U of Michigan, 1890.

_____. "Rhetoric." *International Encyclopedia.* New York: Dodd, 1903.

_____. "What the West Wants in Preparatory English." *School Review* 17 (1909): 10–20.

Scott, Fred Newton, and Joseph V. Denney. *Composition-Literature.* Boston: Allyn, 1902.

_____. *Composition-Rhetoric.* Boston: Allyn, 1897.

_____. *Elementary English Composition.* Boston: Allyn, 1900.

_____. *Paragraph Writing.* Boston: Allyn, 1893.

Smith, Shirley. "Fred Newton Scott as a Teacher." *University of Michigan Senate Collection.* 1935. Ann Arbor: U of Michigan, 1935.

Strauss, Louis. "Regents Merge Two Departments." *Michigan Alumnus* 36 (1930): 331–32.

Thorpe, Clarence. "The Department of Rhetoric." *The University of Michigan, an Encyclopedic Survey in 9 Parts.* 4 vols. Ann Arbor: U of Michigan, 1943: 558–69.

University of Michigan. Board of Regents Proceedings. 1905. Ann Arbor: U of Michigan, 1905.

_____. Calendar of the University of Michigan of 1910–11. *University Bulletin,* New Series, 12, No. 12. April, 1911.

5 A History of Writing Program Administration

Edward P.J. Corbett

The history of writing program administration has all to be recovered, for a complete history of that aspect of collegiate activity does not now exist. Bits and pieces of it exist in various places, and some of it can be reconstructed from the extant histories of other institutions and movements in higher education. Gerald Graff has published his history of literary studies in the United States, *Professing Literature: An Institutional History* (1987). The Southern Illinois University Press has done us a great service with its recent publication of a number of books about the history of teaching rhetoric and composition: James A. Berlin's *Writing Instruction in Nineteenth-Century American Colleges* (1984) and his *Rhetoric and Reality: Writing Instruction in American Colleges 1900–1985* (1987); Sharon Crowley's *The Methodical Memory: Invention in Current-Traditional Rhetoric* (1990); Nan Johnson's *Nineteenth-Century Rhetoric in North America* (1991). And Albert Kitzhaber's forty-year-old dissertation, *Rhetoric in American Colleges, 1850–1900,* with an introduction by John T. Gage, has been published by Southern Methodist University Press (1990). These historical studies illuminate the lineage and the heritage of English departments in this country.

Meanwhile, we can get some idea of the development of collegiate writing programs from Richard Ohmann's *English in America: A Radical View of the Profession* and from Wallace Douglas's chapter in that book, "Rhetoric for the Meritocracy." We get some additional information from a series of articles that Donald C. Stewart has published on the fortunes of writing programs, from some of Robert J. Connors's articles on the textbooks used in freshman composition courses in this country, and from William Riley Parker's classic essay "Where Do English Departments Come From?" A great deal of information about that history can also be inferred from an examination of early issues of the journal *College Composition and Communication*. Of course, if you were associated with English departments right after World War II, either as a graduate student or as a teacher, you can supply some data for that history simply from your own memories of those days. Perhaps the closest thing we have to a history of writing program administration is Susan Miller's recent publication from the Southern Illinois University Press, *Textual Carnivals: The Politics of Composition* (1991).

To begin with, it is well for us to be reminded that writing programs do not belong naturally and inevitably to English departments. This statement from William Riley Parker's "Where Do English Departments Come From?" usually shocks many of our new graduate students and undergraduate majors when they are confronted with it: "Surprising as the idea may first appear to you, there was, of course, no compelling reason at the outset why the teaching of composition should have been entrusted to teachers of English language and literature" (14). English departments inherited the teaching of writing more by default than by divine right. The modern freshman composition course had its beginnings in what happened to the Boylston Professorship of Rhetoric in the last quarter of the nineteenth century. The declining fortunes of the Boylston Professorship and the creation of an English department at Harvard make for an interesting story and help to account for why writing courses became the province of English departments.

Francis James Child, the fourth Boylston Professor of Rhetoric at Harvard, was really more interested in pursuing his interests in literature and philology than in fulfilling his commission as the holder of the endowed chair of rhetoric. In 1869, when Charles William Eliot became president of Harvard, he made it clear that his mission was to convert the university from a preserve for the sons of the privileged classes of New England to a training center for national leaders (Stewart, "Some Facts Worth Knowing" 3). A significant part of that mission was to train a cadre of literate managers and clerks and secretaries for the offices of business and industry. At the time, the most powerful of the humanities departments at Harvard was the classics department, but they had nothing but disdain for courses in writing. If the classics department had been willing to take on the teaching of those writing courses, it might have been able to retain its supremacy in the pecking order of the university and to stave off the threatening rivalry of the other departments. As the esteemed professor of rhetoric, Francis James Child should have been prepared to make a contribution to that mission of enhancing the literacy level of undergraduate students. Instead, he handed over the teaching of rhetoric to his assistant John Dennett and pursued his philological interests. Then in 1876 Child parlayed an offer from the newly founded Johns Hopkins University into the creation of a chair of English literature for himself at Harvard. Adams Sherman Hill forthwith became the fifth Boylston Professor of Rhetoric, an appointment that had dire consequences for the required courses in writing at Harvard and subsequently at other American colleges and universities.

In 1874 Adams Sherman Hill had installed a required course in writing for sophomores, but in 1885 this course was converted into English A, a required course for freshmen, the prototype of the modern freshman English composition course. As a result of a series of pessimistic reports in the 1890s by a Harvard committee charged with assessing the state of student writing, English A was redesigned to concentrate on mechanical correctness and matters of usage in the "daily themes" that Barrett Wendell had mandated for the course (Crowley 12). This preoccupation with mechanical correctness and usage problems made the course drearier and more burdensome than it had been when it was first instituted, and as a result, the professors who enjoyed any stature in the department abhorred the course and did their best to foist the teaching of it off on underlings. Because the faculty of no other department at Harvard wanted to assume the burdens and the ignominy of the writing course, the newly created English department inherited the course by default.

William Riley Parker remarked about this reluctant inheritance, "It was the teaching of freshman composition that quickly entrenched English departments in the college and university structure—so much so that no one seemed to mind when professors of English, once freed from this slave labor, became as remote from everyday affairs as the classicists had ever been. . . . But no one needs to persuade the American public that freshman composition is essential, despite the fact that it rarely accomplishes any of its announced objectives" (13–14). One of the persistent anomalies about the required composition course is that while faculty and students would like to escape from the course, academic administrators and the public will not let them escape. Literacy—at least in the abstract—is highly prized in the United States. There will always be a place somewhere in the university structure for the person who designs, directs, and supervises writing courses for students.

So English departments got saddled with the course in the last quarter of the nineteenth century, and when they carried it over into their curricula in the twentieth century, they turned it into a lackluster service course, not the rich liberal arts course that it might have been if they had made it the kind of rhetoric course that Isocrates and Cicero had designed for their students. As far as one can judge from the syllabi that have survived and from the textbooks used, the course continued to concentrate on matters of grammar, style, punctuation, mechanics, usage, and spelling. And apparently, as long as college enrollments remained small, the program in writing in our colleges could be run as one of the many duties of the head of the department. But the course became a special challenge and burden for English departments when the veterans flocked back to American campuses right after World War II and again in the late 1960s when newly adopted open admissions policies brought a new breed of students to American campuses.

I have been unable to discover from my reading whether early in this century any college English departments in America had such a position as the now familiar director of freshman English. I suspect that in the 1920s, the 1930s, and the first half of the 1940s the composition program was such a relatively small operation in our colleges and universities that, as I suggested above, some factotum in the department could run the program out of his or her back pocket. As an undergraduate student in the early 1940s, I have no memories whatever about my freshman composition course, much less of any office or faculty member within the department that ran the show. Some of the larger tax-supported universities may have had some faculty member appointed specially to direct the writing program, but I have no evidence, either written or oral, that such was the case.

As Leonard Greenbaum's article "The Tradition of Complaint" in *College English* makes abundantly clear, there were frequent questionings of the value of freshman composition throughout the first half of the twentieth century, and from time to time, prestigious members of the profession even called for the abolition of the course. See, for instance, Oscar Campbell's "The Failure of Freshman English" (*English Journal,* March 1939) and Warner Rice's "A Proposal for the Abolition of Freshman English, as It is Now Commonly Taught, from the English Curriculum" (*College English,* April 1960). But although the freshman English course was sometimes changed from a writing course to an introduction-to-literature course, this remained a required course in all but the most highly selective colleges and universities.

Starting in the fall of 1946, however, when tens of thousands of discharged veterans from the armed forces flocked to campuses to begin or to resume their college education, English departments suddenly discovered that they had to set up dozens of additional freshman English courses and to find teachers for those courses. Those swollen enrollments of mature, eager students put severe strains on the resources of the colleges and universities, and they necessitated the creation, among other things, of the office of director of freshman English in the larger schools. So it seems safe to say that the history of writing program administration really begins in the mid-1940s. What I will resort to now is oral history—oral history dredged up from my memories of those days as a graduate student and a beginning teacher.

In the fall of 1946, I and thousands of other discharged veterans of World War II registered for the autumn term at some college somewhere in the United States. We were beginning or resuming either our undergraduate or our graduate education.

We joined the handful of students who were the mainstay of the college campuses during the lean war years — the women and the men who for one reason or another had not become members of the armed forces. Mature beyond our years, we were nevertheless apprehensive about whether we could make it in college, whether we could keep up with the civilian students who had not had to interrupt their education during the war years. But we were eager to learn, and the GI Bill made it financially possible for us to go to college. Many of us became the first member of our family, in any generation, ever to go to college.

That influx of students had profound effects on colleges everywhere. One of those effects is that enrollments in college took a quantum leap, and while enrollments have diminished slightly in the last ten years, they are still considerably higher than they ever were in the prewar years. Another effect is that college faculties had to gear up quickly to accommodate legions of hard-working, no-nonsense students.

English departments especially bore the brunt of that tidal wave of students because, in those days, virtually every college and university required all beginning students to take at least two years of English: a freshman English course and a sophomore survey course in either English or American literature. A veteran just beginning a college education became one of the twenty-five to thirty students who were packed into one of the dozens of newly created sections of freshman English. Because many of the regular faculty of the English department were needed to staff one or more of the required sophomore survey courses, schools had suddenly to find and hire adjunct teachers to teach the bulging composition classes, or if they had a graduate program, they had to dragoon their graduate students into service. So began the tradition of the part-time or adjunct teacher and of the graduate teaching assistant (GTA or TA).

Because I had completed my undergraduate education before I went into the Marine Corps, I began working toward a Master's degree in English in the autumn of 1946. So I did not have to take a freshman writing course or a sophomore survey course in those postwar years, but if I were to become a teacher of English — as I soon decided to do — I would have to prepare myself to teach the freshman writing course and maybe the sophomore survey course. Virtually no English department in the country in those days offered a credit-bearing graduate course in the teaching of composition or literature. But we were prepared in some measure to teach a lower-division survey course because most, if not all, of our graduate courses dealt with literature or literary criticism. But none of our graduate courses prepared us directly to teach a writing course. In fact, many of the veterans who became graduate students in those days never even had a writing course when they were freshmen because they had been exempted from the course. Let me prolong this oral history a bit more to tell you what we did as graduate students or as beginning teachers to prepare ourselves for our writing classes.

Those of you who are old enough to remember those days will nod your heads knowingly as I recount this story; those of you who were too young to remember those days may be slightly incredulous that things could ever have been so bad. Desperation is the word that describes our disposition in those days. We were desperate for suggestions, for guidelines, for approaches, for techniques. We buttonholed our colleagues, pleading for a topic for next week's theme. We wanted tips about how to occupy the fifty minutes of the class period. Should we spend class times doing the drills at the end of each chapter of the handbook? Should we use the opaque-projector to display the best and the worst themes that we got last week? Should we start off every class with a spelling test or a vocabulary quiz? Should we give a split grade on the themes—one for content, one for expression?

Those desperate quests and questions may be familiar even to teachers who have recently joined the ranks. But for those young teachers there are now some ready answers. One ever-ready resource is the rhetoric text prescribed for the course. That kind of text has more information about the writing process than the handbooks that most of us relied on. They also have available to them a syllabus for the course—often a day-to-day syllabus that spells out the assignments and the readings and the theme topics. They have the help of an orientation session at the beginning of the term and of practicums held every week during the term. Behind all those resources — in fact, the person mainly responsible for the availability of those resources — is the director of freshman English, the ultimate recourse when the teacher gets desperate.

It did not take long for schools that offered twenty or more sections of the freshman course every term to realize that they needed a director or a coordinator for the course. Who should it be? The chairperson of the department looked for some industrious, dependable member of the department who showed an unusual interest in, or aptitude for, the teaching of composition. Like the other regular members of the department, this person had the traditional MA and PhD training: a heavy dose of courses in literature and literary criticism (especially the New Criticism), maybe a course in Modern Grammar or the History of the Language, two or three courses in Anglo-Saxon and Middle English, backed up with courses in Beowulf and Chaucer. And of course this person had the requisite reading knowledge of French and German. If this person had any knowledge of rhetoric or composition theory, it was only because he or she had acquired it on the side.

In a talk I gave at an Association of Departments of English (ADE) meeting held on my campus, I said, "One of the glories of our profession in the twentieth century is the legion of freshman directors who took over the onerous and often thankless job of planning a writing program, of setting up practicums to train the writing staff, of visiting the classes of callow teachers, and of fielding the complaints of parents and students. Those gallant men and women saved the day for many English departments." And indeed they did. It was surprising how quickly and efficiently they prepared themselves for their commission. And they soon became a resource for people at other schools who had been appointed to set up and supervise a writing program.

One of the best and most influential of those directors of freshman English was Charles W. Roberts of the University of Illinois at Champaign-Urbana. I recall that I was a member of a general session honoring Charlie Roberts at the 4Cs convention in Louisville in 1967. At the head dais, I was sitting next to Ron Freeman, who had been a TA under Roberts at Illinois. Just before this session was called to order, Ron turned to me and said, "While sitting here, I looked out over this audience, and I counted at least 75 people out there who were TAs under Charlie Roberts in the immediate postwar years and who went on to other colleges and universities and became directors of freshman English—and in some cases, department chairs or college deans." All of you could name other illustrious, influential directors of freshman English, one or more of whom you may have been lucky enough to serve under.

The Conference on College Composition and Communication was founded to serve that growing corps of writing program administrators. More than any other professional organization, the 4Cs is connected with the history of the WPA (Writing Program Administrators). The 4Cs started out in the Midwest, in Chicago, in 1949, and several of the prime movers were from the Big Ten schools. Three of the first set of officers were from Big Ten schools: John C. Gerber, chair, State University of Iowa; George S. Wykoff, secretary, Purdue University; Charles W. Roberts, editor, University of Illinois. (The fourth officer, W. Wilbur Hatfield, was not associated with a university but was the treasurer of the NCTE, with headquarters in Chicago.) Three members of the first executive committee were also from Big Ten schools: Carlton Wells of the University of Michigan, Harold B. Allen of the University of Minnesota; Clyde W. Dow of Michigan State University. Since the October issues of *College Composition and Communication* in those days listed those who participated in the workshops at the annual conventions, one can see when certain well-known figures in composition circles first became involved with the organization. Here are just a few familiar names from those early years: S. I. Hayakawa, Paul Diedrich, John C. Hodges, James McCrimmon, Ken Macrorie, Glenn Leggett, Harry Crosby, Sister Miriam Joseph, Virginia Burke, Priscilla Tyler, Albert Kitzhaber, Albert Marckwardt, Wayne Booth, Karl Dykema, Jerome Archer, Robert Gorrell, Richard Beal. Many of the panels and workshops at the annual conventions dealt with the administration of the freshman English course. If a school could afford to send only one representative to the annual convention, the one who was sent was either the chair of the department or the director of freshman English. Teaching assistants got a chance to attend the convention only when it met in their city. I remember attending my first 4Cs convention at the Morrison Hotel in Chicago when I was a graduate student at Loyola University from 1950 to 1953.

The real professionalization of the composition teacher began after the revival of interest in rhetoric among English teachers. The revival of interest in rhetoric began among speech teachers in the fall of 1920 when Everett Lee Hunt and Alexander Drummond offered a graduate seminar in classical rhetoric at Cornell University. But at the 1961 4Cs convention in Washington, DC, a workshop was offered under the title "Rhetoric — the Neglected Art." Then at the 1963 4Cs convention in Los Angeles, rhetoric suddenly burst on the scene. Several of the panels and workshops at that meeting bore the word rhetoric in their title, and in the October issue of *College Composition and Communication* (*CCC*) that year, the editor, Ken Macrorie, published seven of the papers under the special title "Toward a New Rhetoric." The first Scholars Seminar sponsored by the 4Cs met in December of 1964 at Denver under the leadership of Robert Gorrell, and the subject was rhetoric. The reports of that seminar were published in the October 1965 issue of *CCC* under the special title "Further Toward a New Rhetoric."

Since that time, the interest in rhetoric in composition circles has abated somewhat, but it has never disappeared, and some of the best and the brightest of our young teachers and graduate students have made the study of the old and the new rhetoric their primary professional interest. The 4Cs has also grown in size and in stature, and its journal has come to be recognized as one of the most influential in the field of composition.

But as the 4Cs grew, its interests broadened, and its concern for the administration of the composition course seemed to fade. It was that abatement of interest in the problems of administering the composition courses that prompted a group of 4Cs members to found the organization known as the Writing Program Administrators (WPA). I think I attended what was the first meeting of that group. It was at an MLA meeting in New York in 1976. By that time, the Division on the Teaching of Writing had become one of the new divisions in the restructuring of the MLA and, in fact, had become one of the six largest of the seventy divisions in MLA. Harvey Weiner chaired the meeting, and the room was packed. It was clear from the spirited discussion that ensued that many directors of writing programs felt that a new organization was needed to deal with their problems. A constitution and bylaws were subsequently adopted for the WPA in 1977. Since that time, the WPA has staged special meetings of its members at the annual conventions of the 4Cs, the NCTE, and the MLA. It publishes its own journal, and one of its main functions now is to train a cadre of experienced teachers and directors of writing to serve as consultants and evaluators for college-level writing programs. As far as I know, the conference at Miami University in Oxford, Ohio, 4–8 August 1986, represents the first independent meeting the WPA ever staged.

We might say that the WPA is now fully enfranchised. Since writing courses are more firmly entrenched in the university structure than they have ever been and since the need for professional administrators of writing programs is greater than ever, the future of the Council of Writing Program Administrators is securely cast. The annals of this organization may be short and simple, but before long, those annals will be voluminous and complex.

Works Cited

Archer, Jerome W. "Six-Year History of the CCCC." *College Composition and Communication* 6 (December 1955): 221–23.

Berlin, James A. *Rhetoric and Reality: Writing Instruction in American Colleges 1900–1985.* Carbondale: Southern Illinois UP, 1987.

———. *Writing Instruction in Nineteenth-Century American Colleges.* Carbondale: Southern Illinois UP, 1984.

Campbell, Oscar. "The Failure of Freshman English." *English Journal* 3 (March 1939): 177–85.

Connors, Robert J. "Textbooks and the Evolution of the Discipline." *College Composition and Communication* 37 (May 1986): 178–94.

Crowley, Sharon. *The Methodical Memory: Invention in Current-Traditional Rhetoric.* Carbondale: Southern Illinois UP, 1990.

_____. "The Perilous Life and Times of Freshman English," *Freshman English News* 14 (Winter 1986): 11–16.

Douglas, Wallace. "Rhetoric for the Meritocracy: The Creation of Composition at Harvard." Richard Ohmann. *English in America: A Radical View of the Profession.* New York: Oxford UP, 1976. 97–132.

Gerber, John C. "Three-Year History of the CCCC." *College Composition and Communication* 3 (October 1952): 17–18.

Graff, Gerald. *Professing Literature: An Institutional History.* Chicago: U of Chicago P, 1987.

Greenbaum, Leonard. "The Tradition of Complaint." *College English* 31 (November 1969): 174–87.

Johnson, Nan. *Nineteenth-Century Rhetoric in North America.* Carbondale: Southern Illinois UP, 1991.

Kitzhaber, Albert. *Rhetoric in American Colleges, 1850–1900.* Introduction by John T. Gage. Dallas: Southern Methodist UP, 1990.

Miller, Susan. *Textual Carnivals: The Politics of Composition.* Carbondale: Southern Illinois UP, 1991.

Ohmann, Richard. "English in America, Ten Years Later (with an aside on dechairing the department)." *ADE Bulletin* No. 82 (Winter 1985): 11–17.

Parker, William Riley. "Where Do English Departments Come From?" *College English* 28 (February 1967): 339–51. Reprinted in and quoted from *The Writing Teacher's Sourcebook.* Ed. Gary Tate and Edward P.J. Corbett. New York: Oxford UP, 1981. 3–19.

Rice, Warner. "A Proposal for the Abolition of Freshman English, as It Is Now Commonly Taught, from the English Curriculum." *College English* 7 (April 1960): 361–73.

Stewart, Donald C. "Some Facts Worth Knowing about the Origins of Freshman Composition." *CEA Critic* 44 (1982): 2–11.

_____. "The Status of Composition and Rhetoric in American Colleges, 1880–1902: An MLA Perspective." *College English* 47 (November 1985): 734–46.

_____. "Two Model Teachers and the Harvardization of English Departments." *The Rhetorical Tradition and Modern Writing.* Ed. James J. Murphy. New York: MLA, 1982. 118–28.

Tuman, Myron. "From Astor Place to Kenyon Road: The NCTE and the Origins of English Studies." *College English* 48 (April 1986): 339–49.

Wilson, Gordon. "CCCC in Retrospect." *College Composition and Communication* 18 (October 1967): 127–34.

Part 2

Teaching the Histories of Rhetoric

▼

6

Sapphic Pedagogy
Searching for Women's Difference in History and in the Classroom

Susan C. Jarratt

In Memory of Linda Singer

> . . . we live . . . opposite . . . boldness . . . man
> —Sappho, frag. 24

> Socrates says Eros is a sophist, Sappho calls him a weaver of tales. Socrates is driven mad for Phaedrus by Eros, while Sappho's heart is shaken by Eros like a wind falling on oaks on a mountain.
> —Maximus of Tyre, *Orations*

> I say that even later someone will remember us . . .
> —Sappho, frag. 147

I have chosen these three epigraphs because they introduce themes of gender and difference, learning and desire, and the uses of history.[1] One of the goals of our volume is to show how historical work can be of value to today's teachers of writing. I turn to Sappho because she was the first woman's voice from a Greek heritage that gave us rhetoric. Her fragment 24 marks in its own bold though broken strokes a difference of woman from man. As feminists today ask what difference gender makes in the writing classroom, we may find not answers but echoes of alternative possibilities in Sappho's earliest explorations of this difference. The contrast posed by Maximus of Tyre speaks of the passion for which Sappho is most famous. Like Socrates with his student Phaedrus, Sappho grappled with desire for young companions.

Though the evidence is not clear, it seems possible that this sixth-century BC lyric poet from Lesbos may have been a teacher of young women. If Sappho could be an example, an historical analogue, for women teaching, what are we to do with the woman-inspired Eros for which she is so famous? Would she serve only as a source for Lesbian teaching? Socrates, despite the homoeroticism of "his" (Plato's) language and the homosexual activity acceptable during his time, has persisted for centuries as a model of ethical and rigorous teaching. In this essay I make a case for imagining Sappho as a teacher of women and use that construction as a way of reflecting on the question of difference in feminist theory and teaching.

Sappho as a Teacher

When I began looking closely at sources on Sappho, I was surprised to find that there are no specific references to teaching in her fragments or in the ancient biographies of her (Snyder 12), and yet I had always thought of her as a teacher of women. Perhaps that impression speaks of my (our?) hunger for images of ourselves from the past. Several elements in Sappho's poetry point toward something like a school setting. First, some lines refer to an audience of women— "and now I shall sing this beautiful song to delight the women who are my companions" (frag. 160).[2] One of the visual representations of Sappho pictures her reading poetry for a group of women (see Snyder 6). This representation could suggest a group of peers, but several poems describe younger women. Among them is fragment 49 wherein the narrator admits, "I loved you, Atthis, long ago . . . You seemed to me to be a small and graceless child" (see also frags. 102, 121, and 131). Another group of fragments are hymeneal: poems for women about to be married (frags. 105a, 111, 113, among others). And some poems concern the speaker's pain on the occasion of women departing. Fragment 16 is a priamel, a sort of poetic exercise in induction, which refers to "Anaktoria, who is not here"; fragment 94 may dramatize more explicitly a scene of a young woman leaving the intimacy of close relationship with an older woman/teacher and a group of agemates:

> . . .
> Weeping many tears she left me,
> Saying this as well:

. . .
"Sappho, I don't want to leave you!"
I answered her:
"Go with my blessings, and remember me,
for you know how we cherished you."[3]

These elements together might suggest that Sappho had some responsibility for training groups of younger women prior to marriage. Some scholars in the past have drawn this conclusion, but their apparent reasons for doing so may say more about their own society and its values than about Sappho. Jane McIntosh Snyder notes that an anonymous writer of a tenth-century text made Sappho into a teacher to assure himself of her respectability despite the homoeroticism of her poetry. The reasoning is that if she were a teacher, she must have been totally asexual (12). For the venerable German classicist, U. von Wilamowitz-Moellendorff, seeing Sappho as the leader of a religious cult worked the same way: it made respectable the homoeroticism of her poetry (see also Hallett 451).

Classicists today doubtless have their own limits of vision about Sappho (many of which I wouldn't be able to see), but they do not require a rationalization to explain away the expressions of passion toward other women within a pedagogical framework. Judith Hallett describes Sappho as "a poet with an important social purpose and public function: that of instilling sensual awareness and sexual self-esteem and of facilitating role adjustment in young females coming of age in a sexually segregated society" (450). Marilyn B. Skinner also alludes to a "sex-segregated" subculture, assuming without question the context of a *thiasos,* an all-female religious guild, serving as a "socially sanctioned framework for organizing private and exclusively female experience," as well as teaching "correct womanly behavior within a patriarchal milieu" (5). In a third study, Jack Winkler's reading of gender-consciousness in Sappho's poetry rests on an argument for a public context within which a shared culture is communicated. For his reading, the intimacy of an all-woman audience is more relevant than the relative ages or knowledge of the listeners and speaker (64–65).

Based on these readings and others, I think it is not too far out of line to read Sappho with a question about pedagogy in mind. Snyder and others reveal the Victorian ideology driving previous readings and help direct attention to the purest residue of evidence from antiquity. But they also establish sufficient evidence of Sappho's social context to justify considering her as an analogue for teaching today. Her poetic reflections on difference and desire may bathe our own pedagogical settings in a new/old light.

The Question of Difference

If Sappho can be seen as a teacher, then what can be learned from her about teaching by those committed to transforming the inequities and oppressions based on gender difference? Seeing inequality, feminists in all fields want to do things differently. Feminism has been slow to come to composition teaching, perhaps because the changes wrought by process pedagogies and student-centered practices anticipated in part some of the re-alignments of power and authority that feminists in general seek (see Flynn; Jarratt).

Women may fit more comfortably into composition than into other academic disciplines and other male-dominated professions for several reasons. Most composition classes are small and are offered in the first year of university study; this setting resembles high school, where most of the teachers are women. In them the teacher may consciously or unconsciously take up a maternal attitude toward her students. Many composition theorists currently advise creating an informal and supportive classroom environment with much attention given to student texts and experiences. This pedagogical climate "feminizes" traditional academic practices (Miller)—a feminine difference some see as positive.

But others see less promise in the supportive, nurturing composition classroom for the female teacher. Already in a relatively less powerful position in terms of gender than her male students, the female teacher of a student-centered composition classroom is caught in a contradiction. She stands at the intersection of institutional and gender power axes. Dale Bauer, Patricia Bizzell, bell hooks, and I have all argued for a *feminist* pedagogy of difference from the *feminized* classrooms that challenge institutional authority. The question now becomes a question about *that* difference. How fair is it to allow women—feminists—to practice an authority we would deny to men? Does it circle around to become the same kind of authority formerly held by male teachers within a masculinist institution? Is this not an example of inequality, which we are trying to get rid of? These are arguments I have heard in opposition to the idea of the authoritative feminist teacher—arguments to be countered by a look at recent work in feminist theory.

The question of difference is an important and pressing one for feminist theory. Joan Wallach Scott addresses the theoretical question through an analysis of a contemporary sex discrimination case against Sears, using deconstruction to break open the "difference dilemma." In the suit brought against the giant retailer, the Equal Employment Opportunity Commission (EEOC) charged that Sears was discriminating against women by hiring and promoting more male employees into sales commission jobs. Sears claimed that women did not want these positions because of their "fundamental difference" from men. Women had not pursued these jobs in the past; thus they are "different," and that difference justifies unequal representation in the higher paying jobs. The hiring figures did not evidence discrimination, the defense position implied, because "difference" is categorically and universally opposed to "equality."

Scott's reading of the testimony by prosecution witness, Alice Kessler-Harris, emphasizes the way she contextualizes the categories. "Equality" is not satisfied by a "proof" of difference in past employment patterns; it is only achieved by basing practices on a presumption that women and men might have equal interest in such jobs (139–40). Difference must be contextualized: specific differences for different times and places (142). The fact that women had not sought the higher-paying sales commission jobs was not evidence of a universal and timeless difference on which to base future hiring practices. The employment statistics revealed a socially constructed and histor-

ically located difference, not "fundamental differences" justify-
ing inequality in practices or normative judgments about men's
and women's behavior.

This case demonstrates the necessity that feminist theory
interrupt the opposition of equality-versus-difference as complete, opposed, and mutually exclusive categories. Scott argues
that feminists must move beyond the classifications of various
feminisms on the basis of pure foundations of women's "difference" (labeled variously *lesbian, separatist, radical,* or *cultural
feminism*) or women's "equality" (*liberal feminism*) and shape
politics and practices on an understanding that equality and
difference only exist within each other. Differences imply norms
that must be stated and positions that must be identified. Equality is not sameness. Scott argues, finally, for an end to the
opposition by a focus on differences "as the condition of individual and collective identities, differences as the constant challenge to the fixing of those identities, history and the repeated
illustration of the play of differences, differences as the very
meaning of equality itself" (144). But Scott is not advancing a
radical pluralism, celebrating difference in itself. She recom-
mends a two-stage process for politics and history-writing: first,
"a systematic criticism of the operations of categorical difference, the exposure of the kinds of exclusions and inclusions—the
hierarchies—it constructs"; and second, the movement away
from such an operation of permanent Truth and toward an
equality that rests on differences (146).

I have presented Scott's argument in detail because I think it
helps us understand how a feminist pedagogy can be both
different and equal. Sappho's poems lyrically speak about two
areas of gender difference/equality especially sensitive in teaching relationships: power and passion.

Sappho and Socrates: Power, Passion, Pedagogy

I return here to the passage from Maximus of Tyre. The difference he marks implies a sameness; both Socrates and Sappho
experience erotic feelings for their students (assuming the reference to Phaedrus as a student applies to the case of Sappho).

Plato's dialogue *Phaedrus* deals directly with love and passion in an argument about truth (the Real) and rhetoric. The narrative creates tension through competition between two teachers for a desirable student; it is easy to read in the philosophical arguments about love and lovers the teachers' own desires. The sexual innuendo throughout the dialogue reinforces this message. Socrates tries to peek under Phaedrus's gown to see the scroll he has hidden there. Phaedrus playfully threatens violence against Socrates.

That homosexuality was sanctioned in ancient Greek society is now well accepted. Kenneth Dover, Michel Foucault, and others have described a common pattern of desire among Greek men: an older man takes the active role in pursuing a younger man, who is a passive partner in the sexual encounter. But Plato provides a set of social constraints around sexual relationships in *Symposium* (216d–19d) and *Phaedrus* (238d–41d; 244a–27b). Though passionate desire and admiration for the young student is acceptable, actually engaging in sexual intercourse demonstrates a weakness on the part of the teacher, who should control his desire, and jeopardizes the psyches of both teacher and student.

Today, though homosexual relations are much less acceptable among the majority in Anglo-American cultures, the support, affection, and bonding that undergird academic mentoring relationships still thrive within a homosocial context. This academic tradition has been labeled "filiation" by Edward Said; in more colloquial language, it is the "good old boys" network. These terms do not signify secret longing by male teachers to have sexual relations with young male students, or that sexual desire is the primary motive force in pedagogy. Rather the terms signify the fraternal affective structure of academic life: the comfort men experience in same-sex groups, the tendency to discover and nurture promising students who are male.

Where do women fit into this kind of pedagogical system? The work of Roberta Hall on women in the academy has revealed in some detail how this system affects female students. In some cases they are simply squeezed out; in others, the sexual undercurrent can be easily transferred from male to female student, and even more easily expressed by a male teacher in a heterosexual society. The female student becomes passive recipient of the teacher's loving attention. But for the female teacher, stepping into the Socratic role more radically challenges gender and familial narratives. If our Greek heritage has well served some of us by providing a narrative of "mentoring," might we turn again to that heritage to find an alternative that includes women? How would that cultural formation be different?

Feminist classicists have turned to Sappho to recreate her difference in terms other than those of their nineteenth-century predecessors. They challenge the assumptions of madness, radical idiosyncrasy, or corruption that set the terms of previous explanations.[4] These scholars arrive at new ways of understanding Sappho's sexuality by way of providing a fuller and more complex explanation of the social context for her work: its audience, its settings, its cultural function, and its intertextual relationships to other literature. In several of the studies, there is a strong desire to emphasize Sappho's difference. Hallett, for example, marks difference on the axis of hetero/homosexuality. She reaffirms Page's observation that Sappho did not describe specifically sexual acts between women; rather, the poet "evinces a 'lover's passion' toward other women and give[s] utterance to strong homosexual feelings" (454). Others patrol the boundary between male and female eros, concerned with problems of power and domination. For Skinner, erotic relations between the Sapphic speaker and the beloved are "ideally reciprocal and egalitarian" (6). She asserts egalitarianism in Sappho's thiasos and denies an eros of domination. Eva [Stehle] Stigers, likewise, discovers in Sapphic erotics "mutuality rather than domination and subjection" (56). Sappho's problem as a poet is to describe a different kind of sexuality: "the poetic reason for the inappropriateness of the male pattern to Sappho is that the implicit metaphors of recurrent prostration, domination, and release are based on male sexual psychology, the man's sense of his action in sexual encounter. In order to make aesthetically integrated, convincing love poetry Sappho had to find (or make use of) patterns based on metaphors of female biology and psychology" (50). [Stehle] Stigers uses the *Hymn to Aphrodite,* the only complete poem among the fragments, as the fullest illustration of this erotic difference. She does not find an erotics of domination in the Aphrodite poem, but instead the possibility that the other woman (the object of the poet's desire) could have initiated the relationship. To enter into love, two women "must be equals, each understanding the other from insight into herself" (51).

It is really difficult to see how [Stehle] Stigers can read such difference into the Aphrodite poem. In it, the speaker, named Sappho, calls on Aphrodite to come to her aid. Aphrodite responds, first in indirect discourse asking "Sappho" "what in [her] heart's madness [she] most desire[s] to have." The goddess of love then speaks directly to the poet:

> Whom now must I persuade to join your friendship's ranks? Who wrongs you, Sappho?
> For if she flees, she shall soon pursue; and if she receives not gifts, yet shall she give; and if she loves not, she shall soon love even against her will. (frag. 1)

The poem ends with "Sappho" calling on Aphrodite to be her *summachos,* translated most literally as "fellow-fighter."[5]

These critics have done invaluable work in reassessing Sappho's poetry for the male-dominated field of classics within a thoroughly heterosexist culture. I see in their search for Sappho's difference the desire to remake masculinist culture from the inside out. But how can a reader ignore the desire for power of the lover over the beloved in fragment 1? Persuasion is linked to pursuit and coercion: "she shall soon love even against her will." This linkage is reminiscent of the connections Gorgias makes among love, force, fate, and persuasion in the "Encomium of Helen." In a later article, Stehle offers a more richly nuanced reading of sexuality in Sappho's lyrics, finding that the poet "creates . . . open space for imagining unscripted sexual relations" rather than establishes a gendered difference (108).

I think the desire for radical difference in readings of Sappho is parallel to the anxiety over women's authority in the classroom today. To claim authority is to step across a line of gender difference. This anxiety is expressed in the current distress over "politicizing" the classroom as well. Instead of a value-neutral exchange of information, we have to contemplate the way students may be "influenced": persuaded to change the ways they think about the world in fundamental ways. But even in the humanist educational tradition, hasn't such transformation a goal? To contemplate the best that has been thought and said must surely be assumed to have some transformative, humanizing power. What neutralizes that power is the stability of the social order around its operation. The world is now organized around the values carried by those great works: an essential human nature, self-evident reason, individual autonomy, and free will. Urging students to rediscover those values in literature and reproduce them in their writing is a hegemonic process. The authority of the feminist teacher, however, is counterhegemonic when she argues for the gendered construction of "human natures," culturally specific forms of reasoning, and multiple determinants of subjectivity. Hegemonic authority feels "natural"; its operation is normalized within institutions like schools. But a transformative authority, one calling for change in the fundamental order, calls attention to itself. An analysis that demonstrates what is equivalent but different in these two operations moves feminist theory and pedagogy beyond the "difference dilemma." Readings of Sappho that emphasize her difference have a vital importance within certain discursive and academic terrains. Here, however, I propose that readings exploring what Scott termed "difference as the very meaning of equality itself" can carry further our understanding of feminist authority in the classroom.

Jack Winkler offers a way to understand Sappho's eros as both similar to and different from male desire in her own era. Unlike Page, Winkler locates Sappho's "world" both inside and outside the male sphere. He reverses the figural representation of women's small, domestic "circle" inside the larger male world, arguing instead that "Because men define and exhibit their language and manners as *the* culture and segregate women's language and manners as a subculture, . . . women are in the position of knowing two cultures where men know only one" (69, emphasis in original). His argument is similar to that made by bell hooks that members of minority cultures have to be bilingual, able to speak within two worlds, rather than excluded from the dominant culture. Winkler uses a phrase from one of Sappho's own fragments to describe the gender-consciousness of woman in a male-dominated society. She has a "double mind" (frag. 51) as "one whose consciousness was socially defined as outside the public world of men," but whose female sphere partook totally in that public (65).

Within an all-woman culture, Sappho's "gender-consciousness" includes intimacy, affection, warmth—many features missing in the male world, specifically the world of the Homeric epic. Winkler reads several of Sappho's poems intertextually with their "partners" or equivalents in Homer, showing difference within equality.[6] In a poem echoing the meeting of Odysseus and Nausicaa (frag. 31; *Odyssey* 6.158–61), Winkler shows how the Sapphic speaker takes both roles: the innocent maiden and the exposed, experienced adventurer. The poet, says Winkler, is "masterfully in control of herself as victim. The underlying relation of power then is the opposite of its superficial form: the addressee is of a delicacy and fragility which would be shattered by the powerful presence of the poet unless she makes elaborate obeisance, designed to disarm and, by a careful planting of hints, to seduce" (74).

Here is an erotics of both submission and domination, of domination through submission: the "difference as the very meaning of equality itself" Scott calls for. Sappho is not simply reenacting a sexuality of domination within her own sphere, but neither is she immune to the power of eros. Nor is she blind to her own power as a poet, teacher, and woman. Returning to the passage from Maximus of Tyre, we compare eros as sophist— tricky persuader—to eros as a weaver of tales. The two are not mutually exclusive: tale-tellers try to persuade; sophists tell tales and persuade. Both have a tenuous relation to philosophic "truth," but both speak cultural truths. Socrates is driven mad; Sappho shaken like an oak (frag. 47). Again the experiences are equivalent without being the same. Both feel powerful passion, but madness takes the male philosopher out of the world of illusion and into the vaults of heaven, while the oak remains rooted in the world of nature. Coming to terms with the eros in Sappho's poetry breaks us out of binary oppositions. It suggests the need for a new language, a refiguration of women's experiences of institutional and interpersonal power. How might that authority be characterized outside the confines of different/equal binary?

Speculations on Sapphic Pedagogy

Using Sappho as an analogue for women in the classroom today might make some of us nervous. My point is not to structure the writing class around female homosexuality, nor to sanction sexual contact between students and teachers of any sexual orientation. Rather, I am persuaded by reading Sappho to acknowledge that learning involves currents of erotic desire and exercises of power, no less if a woman teaches than a man. To purge our teaching of the undercurrents of sexuality would be to rob it of a vital energy. I have come to see this paradoxically through discussions—actually, heated arguments in some cases— with male faculty members about sexual harassment. Some male teachers claim that those who wish to protect female students from unwanted attentions of male faculty are really "prudes" who want to deny any form of sexuality in the pedagogical scene, any pleasure or desire animating teacher/student relations. In arguing against that position, I find myself contemplating the invigorating, enlivening influence of desire in learning. That passion has been very male-centered so far, but now that more and more women are moving into positions in the academy, what will happen to the pedagogical eros? Will there just be a simple reversal? Will women form homosocial bonds like Socrates and Phaedrus, leaving out the men? Or will the powerful pressure of heterosexuality blind us to that possibility? Sappho reminds us of its presence.

Sappho's passionate reflections on other women, especially younger women, by contrast show the limitations of the maternal role, the primary cultural resource for imagining women's power. Maternal power in Western culture is both revered and feared; its erotic potential carries severe constraints. Susan Miller has described the maternal qualities of a "negatively feminized identity" for composition. Created out of the history of English departments, the "covering mythology" of the English teacher, according to Miller, includes the self-sacrifice, dedication, and caring of the mother, along with authority, precision, and "impeccable linguistic taste" (46). Jessica Benjamin places the mother as the victim of male erotic domination, tracing the cause to inadequate differentiation from the mother. Euro-American cultural representations of mature women, though they include the kindly, nurturing mother, also offer a dark side; the power granted to older women has definite limits and can turn ugly in the blink of Medusa's eye.[7] Consider the problematic figure of Hera in Greek mythology (see Slater), the wicked witches and stepmothers in European fairy tales. In our own popular culture, we find responses of fear, hatred, and ridicule repeated with figures like Rosalind Shays from the television series *L.A. Law,* the powerful senior partner who was rejected after she rescued the firm and then dropped down an elevator shaft to her death.

With the first wash of the second wave, women joined together under the banner of sisterhood. But in the undertow, feminists began to realize the limitations of "sisterhood" as a feasible or desirable goal for women and have made some tentative steps toward exploring the hazardous territory of power differences among women. Helen Moglen and Evelyn Fox Keller, teacher and student, wrote about the limitations of the family narrative for women within the academy: We could be too-good mothers, never-grateful-enough daughters, or rival-but-loving sisters.[8] Sappho offers an alternative to those roles: a women's community, laced through with power and desire, affection and loss, celebration and beauty, separate from but also within a male-dominated society. Few women teach in all-female institutions, but the insights offered by gendered readings of Sappho's difference-within-equality are as worthy of mining as her Socratic counterpart's for structures of pedagogical identity. My aim is not to model classrooms on the sketchy sense we have of the real circumstances of Sappho's life, but to offer up this scenario for imaginative rumination. To put into circulation another narrative, another possible world.

What difference might this new teaching narrative make? It would insist that we think beyond equality-versus-difference when describing women's power and authority. Without denying a supportive and nurturing role, it suggests the possibility of new combinations.[9] Because Sappho evokes moments of equality, of mutuality of desire, along with the urge to dominate, Sapphic pedagogy does not simply fall back into the male pattern. It participates in it, with a difference. It provides both a caution and an opening. It suggests that psychoanalytic modes of interpretation may have major contributions to make to our understanding of pedagogy, but also that there are terrains of women's experience not taken up by a Freudian paradigm. It suggests a strong basis for connecting lesbian/feminist theorizing with pedagogical projects. Finally, Sappho reminds us that history is not static but a process of continual recreation: "Even later someone will remember us."

Notes

1. Fragment numbers are references to E. Lobel and D. Page, *Poetarum Lesbiorum Fragmenta* (Clarendon: Oxford UP, 1955). All translations are from this text unless otherwise indicated.

2. I wish to thank Marjorie Curry Woods for the phrase "learning and desire," the title of a course she created, and for sharing ideas about the issues taken up in this essay.

3. Translation by Jane McIntosh Snyder.

4. See Page (140–42) for a passage quoted from John Addington Symonds's *Studies of the Greek Poets* (1873) to get a flavor of Victorian interpretations of Sappho. Symonds writes of the "bitter and rotten" fruit of her literary period and of Lesbos as "a mere furnace of sensuality, from which no expression of the divine in human life could be expected." Page himself scrupulously resists drawing conclusions regarding Sappho's sexual activities; he seems to "manage" her sexuality by repeatedly insisting on the poet's detachment (e.g., 16) and the private nature of her circle and her art (e.g., 119).

5. Page translates *summachos* as "comrade-in-arms"; Winkler, as "ally."

6. Page duBois performs a similar interpretive analysis on fragment 16, arguing that Sappho's ascription of agency to Helen alters the traditional narrative structure of the epic. DuBois's analysis that the poem participates in the development of abstract logic while constituting an alternative narrative structure might constitute another example of a reading for difference as the definition of equality.

7. There is an ethnocentrism written into this pronoun "our." I offer these observations about "Western culture" with the reservation that this culture is not one seamless construction and that minority cultures within it may offer more positive alternative figurations of "mother" and "older woman."

8. Kim Tyo-Dickerson's work on this subject has helped my thinking on these issues.

9. Patricia Bizzell suggests the figure of Folly from Erasmus as a possible *ethos* for women in public argument.

Works Cited

Bauer, Dale. "The Other 'F' Word." *College English* (1990): 385–96.

Benjamin, Jessica. "Master and Slave: The Fantasy of Erotic Domination." *Powers of Desire: The Politics of Sexuality.* Ed. Ann Snitow, Christine Stansell, and Sharon Thompson. New York: Monthly Review, 1983.

Bizzell, Patricia. "*The Praise of Folly*: The Woman Rhetor, and Postmodern Skepticism." *Rhetoric Society Quarterly* 22 (1992): 7–17.

Dover, Kenneth J. *Greek Homosexuality.* Cambridge: Harvard UP, 1978.

duBois, Page. "Sappho and Helen." *Women in the Ancient World: The Arethusa Papers.* Ed. John Peradotto and J. P. Sullivan. Albany: SUNY, 1984.

Flynn, Elizabeth. "Composing as a Woman." *College Composition and Communication* 39 (1988): 423–35.

Foley, Helene P., ed. *Reflections of Women in Antiquity.* New York: Gordon and Breach, 1981.

Foucault, Michel. *The Use of Pleasure.* Trans. Robert Hurley. New York: Vintage, 1990. Vol. 2. of *The History of Sexuality.* 3 vols. 1978–90.

Hall, Roberta M. "The Classroom Climate: A Chilly One for Women?" *Project on the Status and Education of Women.* Association of American Colleges, 1982.

Hallett, Judith P. "Sappho and Her Social Context: Sense and Sensuality." *Signs* 4 (1979): 447–64.

hooks, bell. *Talking Back: Thinking Feminist, Thinking Black.* Boston: South End, 1990.

Jarratt, Susan C. "Feminism and Composition: The Case for Conflict." *Contending with Words: Composition in a Postmodern Era.* New York: MLA, 1991.

Keller, Evelyn Fox, and Helene Moglen. "Competition and Feminism: Conflicts for Academic Women." *Signs* 12 (1987): 493–511.

Miller, Susan. "The Feminization of Composition." *The Politics of Writing Instruction: Postsecondary.* Ed. Richard Bullock and John Trimbur. Portsmouth, NH: Boynton/Cook, 1991. 39–53.

Page, Denys. *Sappho and Alcaeus: An Introduction to the Study of Ancient Lesbian Poetry.* Oxford: Clarendon, 1955.

Said, Edward. *The World, the Text, and the Critic.* Cambridge: Harvard UP, 1983.

Scott, Joan Wallach. *Gender and the Politics of History.* New York: Columbia UP, 1988.

Skinner, Marilyn B. "Woman and Language in Archaic Greece, or, Why Is Sappho a Woman?" Unpublished ms.

Slater, Philip. *The Glory of Hera.* Boston: Beacon, 1968.

Snyder, Jane McIntosh. *The Woman and the Lyre: Women Writers in Classical Greece and Rome.* Carbondale: Southern Illinois UP, 1989.

Stehle, Eva. "Sappho's Gaze: Fantasies of a Goddess and Young Man." *Differences* 2.1 (1990): 88–125.

Stigers, Eva [Stehle]. "Sappho's Private World." *Foley* 45–61.

Wilamowitz-Moellendorf, Ulrich von. *Sappho und Simonides.* Berlin: Weidmann, 1913.

Winkler, Jack. "Gardens of Nymphs: Public and Private in Sappho's Lyrics." *Foley* 63–89.

7 Some Techniques of Teaching Rhetorical Poetics in the Schools of Medieval Europe

Marjorie Curry Woods

In the mid-twelfth century, John of Salisbury wrote a famous description of the training in composition used decades earlier by a renowned teacher, Bernard of Chartres.[1] Using a rhetorical mode as familiar now as it was then, John laments that school children are no longer trained as they used to be. But a text written early in the next century, which codifies the twelfth-century developments in the rhetorical composition of Latin verse, shows us otherwise. The *Poetria nova* by Geoffrey of Vinsauf is a text about teaching poetic composition according to the same kinds of rhetorical principles and methods that Bernard of Chartres had used. And the school commentaries that were written on the *Poetria nova* during the next three centuries show that Bernard's teaching methods—such as daily exercises in interpretation, imitation, composition, and recitation—were, in fact, typical for the later Middle Ages, the period during which the great medieval vernacular poets flourished.

Born in about 1115, John of Salisbury was one of the most famous men of his day. Educated in Paris by Peter Abelard, William of Conches, and other noted teachers, John was also a protegé of Thomas á Beckett. After King Henry II's notorious murder of Beckett in 1170, at which John was present, John withdrew discreetly from public life for a time. He was elected Bishop of Chartres in 1176 and remained in France until his death in 1180 (Schultz).

The description of Bernard of Chartres's teaching methods comes in John's *Metalogicon,* a defense of the study of logic that John presented to Beckett in 1159. The first book of this text is about *grammatica,* within which John includes what we would call rhetoric and poetics. For example, chapter 21 begins, "From what has been said, it is clear that grammar is not narrowly confined to one subject. Rather, grammar prepares the mind to understand everything that can be taught in words" (60; 851c).[2]

In chapter 24 of the *Metalogicon,* John describes what he calls, after Quintilian, the *prelectio,* "the intercommunication between teacher and learner (65; 853d)."[3] John quotes Quintilian[4]: "the teacher of grammar should, in lecturing [*prelegendo*], take care of such details as to have his students analyze verses into their parts of speech, and point out the nature of the metrical feet which are to be noted in poems. He should, furthermore, indicate and condemn whatever is barbarous, incongruous, or otherwise against the rules of composition" (66; 853d; quoting *Inst. Or.*, i.8.13ff). John continues:

> He should not, however, be overcritical of the poets, in whose case, because of the requirements of rhythm, so much is overlooked that their very faults are termed virtues. . . . The grammarian should also point out metaplasms, schematisms, and oratorical tropes, as well as various other forms of expression that may be present. He should further suggest the various possible ways of saying things, and impress them on the memory of his listeners by repeated reminders. (66; 853d–54a)

These are general principles, drawn from or based upon the principles of the major rhetorical pedagogue of the ancient world, surprising only, perhaps, in their lack of specific "medievalness."

John also argues for the widest possible background on the part of the teacher: "One will more fully perceive and more lucidly explain the charming elegance of the authors in proportion to the breadth and thoroughness of his knowledge of various disciplines" (66; 854a). And he notes that the great authors give evidence of knowing all of the arts: "Carefully examine the works of Vergil or Lucan, and no matter what your philosophy, you will find therein its seed or seasoning. The fruit of the lecture [*prelectio*] on the authors is proportionate both to the capacity of the students and to the industrious diligence of the teacher" (67; 854c).

For John of Salisbury, then, successful teaching depends on the capacities of both students and teachers. To demonstrate his argument, he describes the specific ways that a legendary teacher (Ward 265), Bernard of Chartres, taught this classical method: tirelessly and always with the capacity of the student in mind. But before examining what John says about Bernard specifically, let us look at the *Poetria nova,* a later text that embodies just the sort of general approach to poetic texts that John advocates. We will see in this text and the commentaries on it some of the specific methods that John describes Bernard using.

The *Poetria nova* was completed about 1215. It is one of a group of arts of poetry that appeared in response to the emphasis placed upon rhetoric, poetry, and grammar in the schools of the twelfth century. The *Poetria nova* was the most widely copied of these arts. Almost two hundred manuscripts of it have survived, and almost half of these contain commentaries or glosses, most of which were prepared and/or used by teachers.[5] Written by Geoffrey of Vinsauf (also called Geoffrey the Englishman), the *Poetria nova* is a two-thousand-line poem about composing verse according to rhetorical principles, many of which are adapted from the *Rhetorica ad Herennium* (called the *Rhetorica nova*). It was modeled on Horace's *Ars poetica,* often called the *Poetria* during the Middle Ages. The *Poetria nova* combined the concepts of rhetoric and poetics in a way that proved particularly fruitful for medieval teachers.

One way that medieval teachers showed that the *Poetria nova* was an important text was by demonstrating how much knowledge was contained within it (as John did with regard to classical works). The commentators[6] often emphasize the comprehensiveness of the text by noting that it encompasses both the five parts of rhetoric (Invention, Disposition, Style, Memory, and Delivery, numbered below I–V) as well as the six parts of a discourse (the Exordium, Narration, Division, Confirmation, Rebuttal, and Conclusion, numbered 1–6). According to the commentators,[7] the preface to the text is the Exordium (1; lines 1–42). The first section, about planning the text before beginning to write it down, is devoted to Invention (I; ll. 43–86), but it is also the Narration portion of the discourse (2; same lines). The discussion of natural and artificial order concerns Disposition (II; ll. 87–202), but is also the Division section of the discourse (3; ll. 87ff.). The important section on Style (III; ll. 203–1842) encompasses Amplification and Abbreviation as well as the Tropes and Figures and the Theories of Conversion and Determination.[8] The Confirmation portion of the discourse (4) comes at line 1842, followed by the Rebuttal (5) at line 1920.[9] Next are the discussions of Memory (IV; ll. 1969–2030) and Delivery (V; ll. 2031–65). At the end is, of course, the Conclusion (6; 2066ff.).[10]

While this double structure is interesting in and of itself from the perspective of the epistemology of textual taxonomies (an issue that I examine elsewhere),[11] its importance for medieval teachers and students is that it shows Geoffrey of Vinsauf to be both a teacher himself, who uses some of the methods John has described, and an author, whose work is used by the commentators as the basis of their teaching. As one thirteenth-century commentator put it, "it should be said that the author of this book is not only a poet but also a teacher of poets in this book" (*EC* 1588,7[12]). We find in Geoffrey's text, and in the use of it made by medieval teachers, the aspects of rhetorical (that is, grammatical) teaching that John and Quintilian described.

As author, Geoffrey breaks the rules because of metrical necessity, and he does so in the very first line, because the name of the person to whom the text is dedicated, *Innocens,* cannot be put into dactylic hexameter. Geoffrey begins the poem thus: "Holy Father, wonder of the world, if I say Pope Nocent I shall give you a name without a head; but if I add the head, your name will be at odds with the metre" (Nims 15; Faral ll. 1–3) The commentators gloss Geoffrey's development of this theme in the lines that follow so that their students can see how he turns metrical liability into a rhetorical asset:

> 6 BUT DIVIDE THE NAME.[13] He says that, through a figure, namely Tmesis (through which a word is completed after the insertion of a word or phrase), this name can be put into the line.

8 SO YOUR VIRTUE. Just as he compared the complete name to the pope's complete virtue, so here he compares dividing up the name to the division of the pope's virtue, because, just as this name when divided is accepted in the meter, so the pope's virtue divided into many parts is found in many persons, but in none is it found all together. (*EC*)

As John of Salisbury notes, "A departure from the rule that is excused by necessity, is often praised as a virtue, when observance of the rule would be detrimental" (66; 854a). The commentators also, like Bernard of Chartres, point out their author's use of figurative language, such as Tmesis in the example above.

Geoffrey as teacher uses another technique that John praised above: he "suggest[s] the various possible ways of saying things, and impress[es] them on the memory of his listeners by repeated reminders," as in the *Poetria nova*'s famous description of how a poet, like a builder, should plan his work beforehand:

> If a man has a house to build, his impetuous hand does not rush into action. The measuring line of his mind first lays out the work, and he mentally outlines the successive steps in a definite order. The mind's hand shapes the entire house before the body's hand builds it. Its mode of being is archetypal before it is actual. Poetic art may see in this analogy the law to be given to poets: let the poet's hand not be swift to take up the pen nor his tongue be impatient to speak; trust neither hand nor tongue to the guidance of fortune. To ensure greater success for the work, let the discriminating mind, as a prelude to action, defer the operation of hand and tongue, and ponder long on the subject matter. (Nims 16–17; ll. 43–54)

And so forth—this is only the first half of the passage.

Let us look now at John's description of Bernard's specific pedagogical methods for inculcating such knowledge, and how such methods are also reflected in the *Poetria nova* and commentaries on it.[14] John begins:

> Bernard of Chartres, the greatest font of literary learning in Gaul in recent times, used to teach grammar in the following way. He would point out, in reading the authors, what was simple and

according to rule. On the other hand, he would explain grammatical figures, rhetorical embellishment, and sophistical quib-
bling, as well as the relation of given passages to other studies.
(67; 854c–d)

The *Poetria nova* was used rarely, if at all, as an introductory
treatise (Kelly; Camargo, "Rhetoric" 107), and discussion of
grammatical aspects of the text are usually limited to interlinear
glosses that point out the relationship of one word to another. But
the commentators pay a great deal of attention to word choice,
rhetorical embellishment, and the connections between the teaching in the *Poetria nova* and other areas of study or bits and pieces
of general knowledge that the students should learn. For example, here is a gloss on the third word of the poem, *mundi* "of the
world."

> OF THE WORLD, that is, of all things that were in the
> world, namely of those things perceptible to the senses and
> imperceptible to the senses; and then it is an example of Metonymy,
> the container for the contents, and in this way he speaks poet-
> ically. Or OF THE WORLD can mean of a rational creature,
> namely of the angels and men who marvel that your[15] virtue
> surpasses human nature, as is said below. Or OF THE WORLD,
> that is, of man alone. For man, like the world, consists of the four
> elements: he has his body from the earth, his vital humor from
> water, his spirit from air, his warmth from fire. Likewise, he
> consists of four humors, namely of melancholy, whose qualities
> are like those of the earth; of phlegm, which is like water; of
> blood, which is like heat or air; of choler, which resembles fire.
> Whence man was called by the Greeks *microcosmos,* that is, a
> smaller world. (*EC* 1,13–18)

The four humors are introduced not as aspects of the poem itself,
but as aspects of knowledge that the author hints at and that the
teacher takes advantage of. Notice that here, too, the possible use
of a trope is noted, so that students learn to recognize metonymy
in context, long before the *Poetria nova*'s discussion of it (Nims
51–52; ll. 966–1012).
    Returning to John's description of Bernard:

And since diction is lustrous either because the words are well chosen, and the adjectives and verbs admirably suited to the nouns with which they are used, or because of the employment of metaphors, whereby speech is transferred to some beyond-the-ordinary meaning for sufficient reason, Bernard used to inculcate this in the minds of his hearers whenever he had the opportunity. (67–68; 854d)

This passage refers to what is discussed in the *Poetria nova* under the Theories of Conversion ("words are well chosen"; Nims 72–79, ll. 1588–760) and Determination ("adjectives and verbs admirably suited to the nouns with which they are used"; Nims 79–82, ll. 1761–841) and the aspect of figurative language called Difficult Ornament ("speech is transferred to some beyond-the-ordinary meaning"; Nims 43–55; ll. 765–1093).

Another of Bernard's methods was to emphasize the particularly artful aspects of the text under discussion as the basis for future imitation: "He would also explain the poets and orators who were to serve as models for the boys in their introductory exercises in imitating prose and poetry. Pointing out how the diction of the authors was so skillfully connected, and what they had to say was so elegantly concluded, he would admonish his students to follow their example" (68–69; 855b).

An early commentary on the *Poetria nova* that has survived in different versions intended for both younger and older students (*EC* xxviii–xxx) shows definite patterns of citation of classical and medieval authors for specific purposes, depending on the sophistication of the student (Woods, "Classical Examples"). And the *Poetria nova* itself was analyzed as a very artful construction, as in the emphasis in this commentary on Geoffrey's own use of artificial (that is, artful) order: "it behooved him to demonstrate not only those techniques that he had been teaching, but also many like these, so that he might be considered worthy of imitation in all things" (*EC* 1588, 8).

John goes on to state that, "[Bernard] would also inculcate as fundamental, and impress on the minds of his listeners . . . what things are to be commended by facts and what by choice of words; where concise and, so to speak, frugal speech is in order,

and where fuller, more copious expression is appropriate . . ."
(69; 855c).

This statement refers to what Geoffrey calls "Easy Ornament," which is composed of the Figures of Thoughts (John's
"commended by facts"; Nims 60–70; ll. 1230–527) and Figures
of Words (his "by choice of words"; Nims 56–60; ll. 1094–229),
and to the medieval doctrines of Amplification and Abbreviation
(Nims 23–42; ll. 203–736), all of which are discussed fully by
the commentators.

Thus, we find encoded in the structure of the *Poetria nova*
itself and consistently emphasized by commentators many of the
techniques and distinctions in kinds of language that, according
to John of Salisbury, Bernard of Chartres tried to teach to his
students: the difference between troped and figured language,
the methods of adding luster to language; methods of organizing
discourse by means of various patterns of ordering; and the
determination of where and how Amplification and Abbreviation
can best be employed. In fact, in all of the school commentaries
on the *Poetria nova* we see a consistent interest in the same
aspects of rhetorical poetics that John of Salisbury described and
that the *Poetria nova* was written to teach a firm belief in the
value of words; an attention to details of verbal, especially
poetic, craftsmanship; an emphasis on early training; and the
judicious use of literary examples and imitation in developing
aesthetic taste and rhetorical power.

These pedagogical techniques were, of course, comple-
mented by exercises performed by the student. John of Salisbury
states that Bernard of Chartres set daily memorization exercises
for his students that were tailored to their individual capacities:
"Each student was daily required to recite part of what he had
heard on the previous day. Some would recite more, others less.
Each succeeding day thus became the disciple of its predecessor" (68; 854d–55a). A statement by Geoffrey of Vinsauf
about the different senses ("This advice holds good for all the
faculties of sense; it sharpens those that are dull (*obtusos*), makes
pliable those that are rigid," Nims 88; ll. 2004–05) is interpreted
in all of the manuscripts of one commentary to refer to the
different intellectual faculties of individual students:

2004 THIS ADVICE [HOLDS GOOD FOR ALL] THE FACULTIES. Intelligence flourishes differently in different individuals. For some are RIGID (2005) in intellect, who grasp instruction with difficulty; and others are OBTUSE (2005), who understand with even greater difficulty. Some, on the other hand, are FLEXIBLE[16] (2006), who grasp quickly; and some are SHARP (2006), who understand immediately and find out many things by themselves. And on account of this, that is, according to the nature of each, the material ought to be shaped FOR THOSE (2006), namely the rigid and the obtuse, and FOR THESE (2007), that is, the flexible and sharp. (*EC* 2004, 1–4)

John specifies some of Bernard's composition exercises: "A further feature of Bernard's method was to have his disciples compose prose and poetry every day and exercise their faculties in mutual conferences, for nothing is more useful in introductory training than actually to accustom one's students to practice the art they are studying" (70; 856A). The commentators on the *Poetria nova* emphasize that what is learned from this text is applicable to metrical and prose composition, as we shall see in the exerpt from the Barcelona manuscript quoted at some length below. Although examples of student compositions are extremely rare—many of them were conducted orally—a few have survived (e.g., Harbert 3; Haskins;[17] Glendenning; Nelson 66–73; Voigts; Woods, "Teaching of Writing" 84–86).

But we must rely on the manuscripts of the commentaries themselves to convey a sense of the actual classroom atmosphere that was generated by individual teachers. For, while almost all of the commentaries on the *Poetria nova* exhibit the techniques that I have described so far, each still conveys a distinct impression of the individual commentator's method of approaching a text, from which we may be able to infer what might have been his[18] method in the classroom. For example, let us look at two different approaches to the first few lines of the famous section of the *Poetria nova* quoted earlier, in which the invention of poetic material is compared to the preparations for building a house.

Here is my literal rendering of the first five lines of the section: If one has to establish a house, let his impetuous hand not rush into action. The work is thought through first, and the inner man outlines the successive steps in a definite order, and the hand of the heart shapes the whole before the hand of the body shapes it.[19]

The fourteenth-century commentary by Reiner von Cappel, a Dominican who wrote commentaries on a number of basic school texts,[20] has a single marginal gloss on these lines:

> 43 IF ONE HAS TO. He already put the Exordium earlier. Here he executes what he intended by first determining the Narration and the Invention of the material. The Narration differs from Invention, since the Narration is the explication through words of events that have occurred or as if they have occurred [*Rhetorica ad Herennium* 1.4], while Invention is the devising of true or plausible things.[21] [*Rhetorica ad Herennium* 1.3]

Reiner refers here to the aforementioned two-fold structure of the *Poetria nova* as the parts of a discourse as well as the parts of rhetoric. Also, Reiner emphasizes that both Invention and Narration involve telling things "as if they were true" or "plausible," as he demonstrates by means of definitions from the *Rhetorica ad Herennium,* the standard source in commentaries on the *Poetria nova* for definitions of rhetorical terms (cf. *EC, accessus* 6–10 and 19–24).

As befits a teacher specializing in the first readers used by students, Reiner also glosses between the lines of the text individual words or constructions that students might find difficult or unclear. Above "not rush into action" (43) is written "that is, not hurry" (*idest non festinet*). "Impetuous" (44) is glossed "thoughtless" (*inconsulta*); "inner man" (46) is glossed "that is, the intellect" (*idest intellectus*); "shapes the entire house" (46) is glossed "prearranges the material" (*materiam predisponat*), and "before" (47) is glossed "earlier" (*prius*).

In other interlinear glosses in the following lines, Reiner clarifies difficult words or grammatical relationships that could appear obscure in the Latin and that Nims clarified in her translation quoted above. For example, "poesis" in line 48 is glossed with what is used by Nims as its English translation:

"that is, poetic art" (*idest ars poetica*). Several lines further, the pronoun *earum* "of these" (53) is glossed by its referents, "namely, of hand and tongue" (*scilicet manus et lingue*), which Nims supplies as well. In line 54, the Latin *tractetque* "and let it ponder" identifies the subject by person and number only, but Reiner, like Nims, supplies it: "namely, the mind" (*scilicet mens*).

Reiner's major purpose is to clarify the text, to make a complex work easier to assimilate. He summarizes. He replaces abstract or esoteric terms with more colloquial ones. He does not add to or interpret the text.

The other commentary, however, an anonymous one found in a late-thirteenth or early-fourteenth century manuscript in Barcelona, creates the opposite impression.[22] This commentator is intent on finding as much as possible within the text. By showing a dizzying array of possible ways of applying the doctrine of the text, he demonstrates the *Poetria nova*'s wide applicability, which was seen as one of the great strengths of the medieval arts of poetry (Jaffe 79–81; Woods, "Unfashionable Rhetoric" 316–17).

There are several long glosses on the first line of the section, each indicated by a paragraph mark. First is a discussion of the composition of the whole section:

> II.[23] 43 IF A MAN HAS. The author's intention is to distinguish among the five parts of rhetoric where each is carried out, and the work is divided into five parts. In the first he treats Invention, where he says, "if a man has". . . .[24] And thus he begins to lay down the treatise, and first on Invention, which naturally precedes the other parts. But since inventing happens two ways, according to the intellect or the subject matter and according to the words or voice, likewise this part is thus divided into two parts. The first speaks of the invention of the material where he says, "If a man has"; the second, concerning the invention of the words where he says "in the hidden chamber of the mind" (60).[25] This first section is further subdivided: in the first subdivision he uses an analogy at the verse, "If a man has," while in the second, where he says "let the poet's hand not be swift" (50), he adapts the analogy. Thus, say therefore, for

whomever it behooves to build a house, before he rushes into
action, they[26] ought to make an archetype of that very house in
the mind and think on it inwardly: how high? how long? and
where the gate and windows? and with what preparers? Thus,
one wishing to compile a poem should consider in what style he
ought to write, whether low, middle, or grand; what elaborated
topic he can take to what conclusion[27]; and through what method
he ought to return.[28]

Then we read this interpretation of the passage:[29]

A HOUSE is said to have four parts in general. The first is the
foundation, the second is the length, the third is the width, the
fourth is the roof. But these four parts are reduced to three parts,
namely to the foundation and the walls and the roof. And thus a
letter[30] can be reduced to three parts accordingly, for according
to some it is said that the Salutation is not a part of the letter, but a
kind of title illuminating the whole letter.[31] As it is said, even
when the title of a work is erased, the whole page remains
known. And thus according to them the Salutation is not the
principle part of the letter; the same with the Introduction. And
according to the authorities those two [Introduction and Salutation?] generate a letter well, and thus the letter remains [com-
posed] principally of the Narration and the Petition and the
Conclusion. And thus "If one has a house," etc. But there are
others who say that the letter has five parts, and so it is held by
the masses. But, according to the working out of the passage, he
says foundation, that is, Narration; walls, that is, Petition; room,
that is, Conclusion.[32]

Then the commentator lists a series of points, each marked
off as a separate paragraph:

Chapter: IF A MAN HAS A HOUSE, etc. The second
chapter.
The chapter on the Invention of material, up to "In order
that the pen may know" (77).
In this passage, he gives three examples of Invention and of
thinking through the method of the material or of the work.
The first method of thinking through the material or the
work or the letter either in verse or in prose: in the mind.

The rhetorician does five things: he finds, arranges, deco-
rates. And, memorizing, he presents with the "seasoned flavor"
(86) of the voice.[33]
    Man is two-fold, viz. the outer man, that is the body, and the
INNER MAN (46), that is, the spirit, that is, the apportionment
of the spirit. The INNER MAN, that is, the reason or intellect of
the spirit. The outer man, that is, having actions, that is, the
actions after such thinking, that is, the exercise of the pen.[34]

Since this commentator's interlinear glosses are just as
prolific, only those on the very first sentence of the section are
quoted here. (I have inserted the glosses in parentheses after the
phrase or word glossed):

> If one (that is, if some man) has to establish (to build) a
> house (that is to say, if someone has to build something, as a letter
> so a building, either in verse or in prose), let his impetuous hand
> (that is, burning or quick and full of speed, since at first he
> organizes, afterwards advances and makes, that is the building)
> not rush into action (that is, to the deed, that is, to the matter at
> hand, that is, to the building of the house).[35]

Our first commentator, Reiner von Cappel, taught younger
students, while the second commentary is probably intended for
an older audience, although neither of these commentaries agrees
exactly with the paradigmatic stances I have described elsewhere
(Woods, "A Medieval Rhetoric"). But although some of the
differences between these commentaries could be the result of
the age of the student, the very extremeness of each bespeaks a
personal reaction to the text and a powerful yet limited sense of
the best way to convey it.[36] While Reiner's students might have
been bored from time to time, they would not have been confused. They would have known at every moment what they were
learning and why. From the plethora of glosses by the second
commentator, however, we can infer that students taking all this
in might have been confused and even bewildered at times. But at
other times they could have been stimulated and inspired.
    One of these teachers makes simple, the other makes
complex; one reduces, the other amplifies. One marks bound-

aries, the other breaks them. One would have been successful with the "rigid" and "obtuse" students, the other with the "flexible" and "sharp" ones. I infer from John of Salisbury's emphasis on Bernard of Chartres's attention to the capabilities of each student that Bernard used each approach when appropriate. This adaptability was his most impressive pedagogical tool.

Let me conclude with two student reactions to yet another teacher of the *Poetria nova*. These are medieval student evaluations, first the official one, and then another, perhaps by the same person, added unofficially. While most of the manuscript containing them dates from the fourteenth century, the end of the text of the *Poetria nova,* where the "evaluations" occur, is from the fifteenth century.[37]

In the colophon or ownership note at the end, the student states, "This is my book, Johanotus de Georgis, who goes to the school of Professor[38] Euxobus de Uercellis, who is a good teacher of grammar."[39] But underneath has been drawn, either by the same hand or by another offering a conflicting view, a picture of someone being beaten on the shoulders with a stick or some other instrument. Because the person being beaten is raising his index finger as if in instruction or admonishment and because he is wearing a piece of ostentatious headgear, he appears to be the teacher himself, perhaps being treated on parchment as he has treated his student in the classroom.[40] Of course, the colophon may have been dictated, for the marginal illustration indicates critical intent on the part of the illustrator, even if only superficial or momentary (or even imaginary, if written by a later reader or student rather than someone on the scene in the class referred to in the colophon).

Unfortunately, for centuries before and after as well as during the Middle Ages, pedagogical flogging has been considered an efficacious way of teaching the "rigid" or "obtuse" student. Even Bernard of Chartres, John of Salisbury tells us, used it on occasion: "In view of the fact that exercise both strengthens and sharpens our mind, Bernard would bend every effort to bring his students to imitate what they were hearing. In some cases he would rely on exhortation, in others he would resort to punishments, such as flogging" (68; 854d). Regrettably, however, while rejecting flogging, we have also come to view with suspicion the other techniques used to teach rhetorical poetics during the Middle Ages. That a student so gifted as John of Salisbury extravagantly praised the training in the minutiae of language offered by Bernard of Chartres should encourage us to acknowledge such training as potentially useful and stimulating, as a means of enabling the student to have at his or her disposal at an early age the full power of the most important tool of access to dominant culture.[41] That this training was received when the students were young is not necessarily a sign, as it would be today, that it was not valued within the society. We should not let our own post-Romantic training blind us to the ability of pre-modern teachers to teach students to write rhetorically and to analyze rhetorical works, whether in prose or verse, and whether of their own age or an earlier one.

Notes

1. I would like to thank Michael Leff for his encouragement of this project when it was given as a paper at the meeting of the International Society for the History of Rhetoric in Tours, 1987. Catherine Loomis read and commented on an earlier draft. I am particularly grateful to Martin Camargo for suggestions on the portions pertaining to medieval letter-writing manuals and collections.

2. For reasons of space I have not quoted the Latin of edited texts, although I do so for all quotations taken from unedited sources. The standard Latin editions are listed in the bibliography, and the second number in the reference refers to the relevant Latin edition.

3. The prefix *pre-* distinguishes one meaning of *lectio* (reading), "the activity of teaching and being taught," from another *lectio* (reading), "studying written things by oneself" (65, 853b). McGarry translates *prelectio* as "lecture" and *prelegendo* as "lecturing." But it seems to me that John means something more interactive, or at least attentive to specific student situations, than the term *lecture* conveys. The Barcelona manuscript quoted below, however, seems to mean by *lectio* something like "passage," perhaps closer to McGarry's "lecture."

4. On the knowledge of Quintilian in the Middle Ages, see Lehmann; Winterbottom 22–30; and Murphy, Rhetoric 123–30.

5. The standard modern edition of the *Poetria nova* is in Faral 194–262. For earlier editions, etc., see Woods, "Unfashionable Rheto-

ric" 316 and 320, notes 30 and 34. The first translation into English was that by Nims, which along with Faral's edition is used as the basis for quotations here. (At the time of this publication, Nims's translation is available as an inexpensive paperback from the Publications Department of the Pontifical Instiute of Mediaeval Studies, St. Michael's College, University of Toronto.) Other English translations are in Gallo and in *Three Medieval Rhetorical Arts.*

6. When I talk about "the commentators" in general, I am describing approaches to the *Poetria nova* that were widely held. But I give citations from *An Early Commentary (EC)* because it is translated and because it has survived in thirteenth-, fourteenth-, and fifteenth-century manuscripts. Later in this essay, when I cite unedited manuscripts, I also add references to similar statements in *EC* if possible. Recently I published an article in which I make distinctions between the school and university commentaries on the *Poetria nova,* but here I draw on both traditions. I am, however, more interested in the school tradition, which demonstrates the greatest continuity with the school methods of Bernard of Chartres as John describes them.

7. Some of the commentators, including ones quoted later in this paper, identify the divisions as occurring at different lines, but the sequence of topics is consistent.

8. The Theory of Conversions concerns the effect of changing the expression of a concept from one part of speech to another, while the Theory of Determinations concerns verbal ornamentation by means of metaphoric modifiers.

9. Sections 4 and 5 together are called "Various Prescriptions" by Nims (see note 10), but 4 encompasses instructions on Choice of Words and Comic Style, while 5 includes what she calls "Faults to Avoid."

10. By way of comparison, note the divisions of a modern translator of the text, Margaret F. Nims, who is familiar with the manuscript rubrics of the text:

Dedication (ll. 1–42).
I. General Remarks on Poetry; Divisions of the Present Treatise (ll. 43–86).
II. Ordering the Treatise (ll. 87–202).
III. Amplification and Abbreviation (ll. 203–689).
    A. Amplification.
    B. Abbreviation.
IV. Ornaments of Style (ll. 737–1968).

1. Difficult Ornament [tropes].
2. Easy Ornament [figures of words and thoughts].
3. Theory of Conversions.
4. Theory of Determinations.
5. Various Prescriptions (ll. 1842–1968).

V. Memory (ll. 1969–2030).

VI. Delivery (ll. 2031–2065).

Epilogue (2066–2115).

11. "Teaching the Tropes: The Theory of Metaphoric Transference in School Commentaries on the *Poetria nova,*" in progress.

12. The first number is the line number of the *Poetria nova* in which the glossed word is located; the second refers to the sentence numbers within the gloss.

13. The numbers are the line numbers of the *Poetria nova* which I have supplied. The medieval readers relied on the lemmata, or words quoted from the text, to identify the place in the text. These are usually underlined in the manuscripts, but I have capitalized them.

14. For my own rhetorical purposes I have rearranged some of the elements of John's description of Bernard's methods when quoting from it.

15. "Your" (*tua*) refers to Pope Innocent III, to whom the work is dedicated and whose name was impossible to put into the poem for metrical reasons.

16. Here I have emended my translation of *molles* in *EC* from "malleable" because in this context Nims's more positive term seems appropriate. Where my translation of words in this passage differs from Nims's, (e.g., "sharp" for "acute," "obtuse" for "dull"), the Latin term can mean either English one, and both translations are applicable to descriptions of the senses as well as intellectual faculties.

17. A number of medieval collections of sample letters contain examples of student letters to parents, patrons, etc., usually asking for money. In the case of a given letter it is often difficult to know whether it is an actual student composition, a student composition revised by the teacher, or the teacher's own composition. Haskins is still the standard reference on this topic.

18. Assuming that the commentators were all male, I employ the masculine pronoun in its gender-specific sense.

19. It might be useful to have the Latin of this section:

Si quis habet fundare domum, non currit ad actum
Impetuosa manus: intrinseca linea cordis

Praemetitur opus, seriemque sub ordine certo
Interior praescribit homo, totamque figurat
Ante manus cordis quam corporis. . . . (43–47)

20. For information on Reiner, see Sturlese. Loris Sturlese is planning an edition of Reiner's commentaries, including that on the *Poetria nova*.

21. "Si quis habet. Iam premisit exordium. hic exequitur intentum, deter[m]inando primo de narracione et materie inuencione; differt autem narracio ab inuencione, quia narracio est rerum gestarum uel prout gestarum per sermonem explicacio. Inuencio vero est rerum verarum uel verisimilium excogitacio." (Wolfenbüttel, Herzog August Bibliothek Cod. Guelf. 286 Gud. lat., fol. 1v.)

22. Archivo de la Corona de Aragon MS Ripoll 103. I am grateful to Christopher Baswell for help in dating and interpreting this manuscript.

23. The Roman numeral at the beginning of the gloss is also written next to the first line of the section glossed to identify the place in the text.

24. In a short section that I have omitted, the commentator proceeds to identify, according to a structure somewhat different from the one outlined above, where each part of rhetoric is treated.

25. The commentator, as was common practice, quotes only the first few words of the phrase in Latin (which occur in the middle of the English sentence), just enough to identify the line. The complete sentence shows the transition that the commentator is pointing out: "When due order has arranged the material in the hidden chamber of the mind, let poetic art come forward to clothe the matter with words" (Nims 17; ll. 60–61).

26. The Latin changes from singular to plural here.

27. This clause and the next refer to Digression, a method of Amplification (Nims 35–36; ll. 527–54).

28. "II *Si quis habet* etc. Intentio auctoris est discernere de quinque partibus rectorice in ista executiua parte, et diuiditur in quinque partes. in prima tractat de inuencione, ubi dicit *Si quis habet*. . . . et sic incipit tractatum ponere, et primo de inuentione, que naturaliter alias partes precedit. Verum quia contingit dupliciter inuenire secundum intellectum siue materiam, et secundum uerba siue uocem, ideo presens pars ita diuiditur in duas partes. primo dicit de inuentione materie ubi dicit *si quis habet*. secundo de inuenctione uocabulorum ubi dicit *mentis in archano*. Iterum prima subdiuiditur.

in prima ponit similitudinem, uersus siquis habet ["u^{er}. s. h"] in secunda uero ubi dicit *non manus* ponit adaptationem similitudinis. Dic ergo sic quod quemadmodum oportet fundare domus priusquam ad actum currat qualem ipsam domum debent facere in mente si rechetipa [= archetipa] et animo cogitare. quam altam. quam longam. et ubi hostia et fenestras. et quibus preparatoriis [= preparatoribus?]. ita uolens poemata compilare debet considerare quo stilo scribere debeat. vtrum humili, mediocri, uel subblimi stilo. quam prolixam materiam ad quem finem uenire possit et per quem modum debeat remeare" (fol. 1v). This manuscript is worn, highly abbreviated, and very fully annotated; some parts of the transcription and translation are conjectural.

29. There are some indications (spatial arrangement, possible changes in script, etc.) that the section just quoted may be by a later hand. But the cumulative effect is coherent, distinctive, and effective.

30. This application of the *Poetria nova* to the practice of letter writing demonstrates that medieval treatises on composing rhetorical poetry could be applied to specific prose forms (just as the *Rhetorica ad Herennium* and *De inventione* were probably used in teaching the composition of rhetorical verse). See also Camargo, "Comprehensive Art."

31. The reduction of the parts of a letter to three is not that unusual, though the inclusion of the *conclusio* among those three is. See the discussion in Murphy of Boncompagno's failed attempt at setting up a "system of three-part letters" (*Rhetoric* 255), and Alessio's edition of Bene of Florence, *Candelabrum* (e.g., III:4.6, and notes on pp. 335–37).

32. "PP Domus dicitur habere quatuor partes in generali. prima est fundamentum, secunda est longitudo, tertia est amplitudo. quarta est tectum. sed iste quatuor partes reducuntur ad tres partes, scilicet ad fundamentum et ad parietem et ad tectum. et ita epistola potest reduci ractione ad tres partes secundum quid (?). nam secundum quosdam dicitur quod salutatio non est pars epistole, set quidam titulus illuminans totam epistolam, vt dicitur abraso libri titulo, tota pagina remanet certa, et sic secundum illos salutatio non est pars principalis epistole. exordium similiter. et ista duo secundum illos faciunt ad bene esse epistolam. et sic epistola remanet ex narractione et petissione. et conclusione, principaliter. sic et domus habet etc. set alii sunt dicentes quod epistola habet quinque partes et ita tenetur vulgo. set ob actationem lectionis dixit fundamentum, idest narratio, paries idest petitio, tectum idest conclusio" (fol. 1v).

33. A listing of the functions of the five parts of rhetoric, which are summarized in lines 79–86.

34. "PP Capitulum. *si quis habet* etc. Capitulum secundum. "PP Capitulum de inuentione materie. vsque *neu stilus ignoret.* "PP In ista lectione dat tria exempla de inueniendo et premeditando modum materie uel operis.

"PP primus modus de premedatatione materie uel operis, uel epistole uel metrice uel prosaice, in intellectum.

"PP quinque facit rector. reperit, disponit, ornat. Et memorans profert vocis condita sapore.

"PP Duplex est homo, videlicet homo exterior idest corporis, et homo interior idest anima idest discreptio animi. [***] homo interior idest ratio uel intellectio animi. homo exterior idest acta habens idest actus post putationem talem idest exercitio calami." (fol. 1v)

35. "Si quis (idest si aliquis homo) habet fundare (edificare) domum (PP quod dicit, si aliquis habet facere aliquod opus tam edificiale quam epistolare uel metrice uel prosaice), non currat ad actum (idest ad factum, idest ad negotium, idest ad edificationem domus) Impetuosa manus (idest tostana uel cita et plena impetus, quia primitus ordinet postea vadat uel facit, idest edificium)." (fol. 1v)

36. Parts or most of both commentaries could have been, indeed probably were, copied from other manuscripts. Originality is not at issue here (cf. note 29).

37. Turin, Biblioteca Nazionale MS F. IV. II.

38. Grendler notes that "the title *magister* usually prefaced [the names of grammarians who taught at a pre-university level in Florence], while university professors were called *dominus*" (25). This student seems to indicate that both were applicable.

39. "Iste liber est mei iohanoti de georgis qui Vado ad Scollas/domini euxobi de uercellis qui est bonus magister in sua gram[ma]tica." (fol. 41v)

40. Another possible interpretation: a child—albeit a pretentious one or one imitating his teacher—is being beaten.

41. Such teaching methods, some of which still might be of use to us today, began well before the Middle Ages (Murphy, "Modern Value of Ancient Roman Methods of Teaching Writing") and lasted for centuries afterwards (Horner).

Works Cited

Manuscripts

Barcelona. Archivo de la Corona de Aragon MS Ripoll 103. Folios 1r–46v. 13th–14th century.

Turin. Biblioteca Nazionale MS F. IV. II. Folios. 15r–41v. 14th–15th centuries.

Wolfenbüttel. Herzog August Bibliothek Cod. Guelf. 286 Gud. lat. Folios. 1r–36v. 14th century.

Published Works

Ad C. Herennium (Rhetorica ad Herennium). Trans. Harry Caplan. Cambridge: Harvard UP, 1954.

Bene of Florence. *Candelabrum*. Ed. Giancarlo Alessio. Padua: Antenore, 1983.

Camargo, Martin. "Rhetoric." *The Seven Liberal Arts in the Middle Ages*. Ed. David L. Wagner. Bloomington: Indiana UP, 1983. 96–124.

———. "Toward a Comprehensive Art of Written Discourse: Geoffrey of Vinsauf and the *Ars Dictaminis*." *Rhetorica* 6 (1988): 167–94.

An Early Commentary on the Poetria nova *of Geoffrey of Vinsauf.* Ed. and trans. Marjorie Curry Woods. Garland Medieval Texts 12. New York: Garland, 1985. Cited as *EC*.

Faral, Edmond. *Les arts poétiques du xiie et du xiiie siècle: Recherches et documents sur la technique littéraire du moyen âge. 1924.* Paris: Champion, 1962.

Gallo, Ernest. *The* Poetria Nova *and Its Sources in Early Rhetorical Doctrine.* The Hague: Mouton, 1971.

Geoffrey of Vinsauf. Poetria nova *of Geoffrey of Vinsauf.* Trans. Margaret F. Nims. Toronto: Pontifical Institute of Mediaeval Studies, 1967.

Glendenning, Robert. "Pyramus and Thisbe in the Medieval Classroom." *Speculum* 61 (1986): 51–78.

Grendler, Paul F. *Schooling in Renaissance Italy: Literacy and Learning, 1300–1600.* Baltimore: Johns Hopkins UP, 1989.

Harbert, Bruce. "Introduction." *A Thirteenth-Century Anthology of Rhetorical Poems: Glasgow MS Hunterian V.8.14.* Toronto, Centre for Medieval Studies, 1975.

Haskins, Charles Homer. "The Life of Mediaeval Students as Illustrated by Their Letters." *American Historical Review* 3 (1898): 203–29. Revised version in *Studies in Medieval Culture*. Oxford: Clarendon, 1929.

Horner, Winifred Bryan. "Writing Instruction in Great Britain: Eighteenth and Nineteenth Centuries." *A Short History of Writing Instruction from Ancient Greece to Twentieth-Century*

America. Ed. James J. Murphy. Davis, CA: Hermagoras, 1990. 121–49.

Jaffe, Samuel Peter. "Studies." *Nicolaus Dybinus'* Declaracio oracionis de beata Dorothea: *Studies and Documents in the History of Late Medieval Rhetoric*. Beiträge zur Literatur des XV. bis XVIII. Jahrhunderts 5. Wiesbaden: Steiner, 1974.

John of Salisbury. *Ioannis Saresberiensis Episcopi Carnotensis Metalogicon*. Ed. Clemens C. I. Webb. Oxford: Clarendon, 1929.

————. *The* Metalogicon *of John of Salisbury: A Twelfth-Century Defense of the Verbal and Logical Arts of the Trivium*. Trans. Daniel D. McGarry. Berkeley: U of California P, 1955.

Kelly, Douglas. "The Scope of the Treatment of Composition in the Twelfth- and Thirteenth-Century Arts of Poetry." *Speculum* 41 (1966): 261–78.

Lehmann, Paul. "Die Institutio oratoria des Quintilianus im Mittelalter." *Philologus* 89 (1934): 349–83. Rpt. in *Erforschung des Mittelalters: Ausgewählte Abhandlungen und Aufsätze*. 4 vols. Leipzig: Hiersemann, 1941–59. 2: 1–28.

Murphy, James J. "The Modern Value of Ancient Roman Methods of Teaching Writing, with Answers to Twelve Current Fallacies." *Writing on the Edge* 1 (1989): 28–37.

————. *Rhetoric in the Middle Ages: A History of Rhetorical Theory from Saint Augustine to the Renaissance*. Berkeley: U of California P, 1974.

Nelson, William, ed. *A Fifteenth-Century School Book from a Manuscript in the British Museum (MS. Arundel 249)*. Oxford: Clarendon, 1956.

Schultz, Janice L. "John of Salisbury." *Dictionary of the Middle Ages*. Ed. Joseph R. Strayer. 13 vols. New York: Scribner's, 1982–89. 2: 139b–40b.

A Short History of Writing Instruction from Ancient Greece to Twentieth-Century America. Ed. James J. Murphy. Davis, CA: Hermagoras, 1990.

Sturlese, Loris. "Der Soester Lektor Reiner von Cappel O.P. und zwei Wolfenbütteler Fragmente aus Kapitelsakten der Dominikanerprovinz Saxonia (1358, ca. 1370)." *Wolfenbütteler Beiträge* 6 (1983): 186–201.

Three Medieval Rhetorical Arts. Ed. James J. Murphy. Berkeley: U of California P, 1971.

Voigts, Linda. "A Letter from a Middle English Dictaminal Formulary in Harvard Law Library MS 43." *Speculum* 56 (1981): 575–81.

Ward, J. O. "The Date of the Commentary on Cicero's 'De Inventione' by Thierry of Chartres (ca. 1095–1160?) and the Cornifician Attack on the Liberal Arts." *Viator* 3 (1972): 219–73.

Winterbottom, Michael. *Problems in Quintilian.* University of London Institute of Classical Studies Bulletin Supplement 25. London: Institute of Classical Studies, 1970.

Woods, Marjorie Curry. "Classical Examples and References in Medieval Lectures on Poetic Composition." *Allegorica* 10 (1989): 3–12.

_____. "A Medieval Rhetoric Goes to School — and to the University: The Commentaries on the *Poetria nova.*" *Rhetorica* 9 (1991): 55–65.

_____. "The Teaching of Writing in Medieval Europe." *Short History.* 77–94.

_____. "An Unfashionable Rhetoric in the Fifteenth Century." *Quarterly Journal of Speech* 9 (1989): 312–20.

8

Dialectics and Rhetoric in Renaissance Pedagogy

Jean Dietz Moss

Ever since the appearance of Father Walter Ong's *Ramus: Method and the Decay of Dialogue,* teachers of rhetoric and composition have been made aware of the decline of the ancient study of dialectic.[1] Taking its origins from the kind of dialogue employed by Socrates and Plato, *dialectics,* as the scholastic discipline is often termed, was developed by Aristotle into a dynamic heuristic and systematic form of debate, which became the method of inquiry in all the sciences from astronomy to metaphysics. Now John Nelson, Allan Megill, and Donald Mc-Closkey proclaim the ubiquity of the *rhetoric* of inquiry and of persuasion in the human sciences (3–18), while Alan Gross would extend rhetoric's realm to include that of the "hard" sciences as well (3–20).

In light of the historical picture depicted in Ong's book and the claims of more recent writers, those of us who teach the history of rhetoric may wonder if the first sentence of Aristotle's *Rhetoric,* where he declares that "Rhetoric is a counterpart (*antistrophos*) of Dialectic," has not lost all meaning for the teaching of rhetoric today. Perhaps an examination of actual teaching texts that preserved these distinctions may illuminate the nature of both of the arts and help us to understand the significance of Aristotle's comparison. Certainly, in these distinctions also lie implications (and "special topics") for the epistemological and axiological debates about rhetoric in our era, which should become apparent during the exposition that follows— even though there is not space to develop them in detail here.

For this tribute volume to Winifred Horner, I have focused on two Renaissance texts that analyze the nature of both dialectics and rhetoric, demonstrating the differences and similarities of these two arts. My hope is that these works may suggest additions to our continued "appropriation" of classical principles of discourse for the teaching of modern rhetoric and composition.[2]

The scholars to whom I turn for guidance are Ludovico Carbone and Antonio Riccobono. Carbone was an influential teacher in Ferrara and Perugia whose writings were well known in the late Renaissance. Incorporating the teachings of his professors at the Collegio Romano, the flagship Jesuit college at Rome, he turned out numerous writings on rhetoric, logic, philosophy, and theology, which were published in the last two decades of the sixteenth century.[3] At about the same time Antonio Riccobono was lecturing on rhetoric at the University of Padua. He published his translation and commentary on Aristotle's *Rhetoric* in 1579.[4] Both Carbone and Riccobono were known in one way or another to the Father of Modern Science, Galileo Galilei. Carbone's works on logic were appropriated by Galileo in his, until recently, unpublished manuscript on logic, and Riccobono was teaching at Padua when Galileo arrived there as a young professor.[5] Whether his views on rhetoric influenced Galileo is unknown, but the two corresponded even before Galileo's arrival at Padua.[6]

Rhetoric According to a Renaissance Commentator

Riccobono's discussion of the nature of rhetoric highlights the art's similarity to and difference from dialectics, and since we are most familiar with rhetoric today, his text provides a good starting point. In his commentary on Aristotle's *Rhetoric* the Paduan professor stays close to the text, which he translates in the first 198 pages of the book, but his aim is to clarify by approaching the work in what he calls a philosophical manner, dividing the matter by appropriate headings and examining each of these in detail. In this way he hoped, no doubt, to make Aristotle's text more accessible to his students and to provide them with what he thought to be the best thinking on these matters drawn from ancient and modern commentators. Surprisingly, Riccobono refers throughout to the opinion of contemporary Italian scholars on Aristotle's *Rhetoric,* thereby indicating that this work was a far more common subject of study in the universities of Northern Italy than has hitherto been recognized.[7] The interweaving of the Aristotelian logical tradition with Humanist academic interests is a common characteristic of these writings.

Following the philosophical and pedagogical practice of the day, Riccobono is first intent upon developing a definition of rhetoric (201). He searches for the proximate genus of rhetoric and then for its differentia. He allows that although it does belong within the genus of art, more proximately it falls within the genus of faculty, as Aristotle indicates in his analysis. Dialectics also belongs to that genus, he notes. Riccobono points out that "faculty" is not meant here in the general sense, the power to do something or contemplate something, which could be attributed to all disciplines, but a specific facility is intended, the power to "demonstrate contraries." Such a power belongs only to these two arts (203–04). Other arts, he explains, may be concerned with contraries also, but these are ordered to establishing one contrary over another, as when the doctor desires to bring his patient from sickness to health. The arts of rhetoric and dialectics, however, seek to find arguments bearing on both contraries equally.

To discern its differentia, Riccobono considers rhetoric's purpose or end. He takes issue with Quintilian, who thought that to speak well was the rhetorician's end, and says that his "true end" is to persuade. An end, for Riccobono, must be the ultimate aim to which all others are ordered. In that sense to speak well is only a means toward rhetoric's end. Furthermore, he points out that ends may be thought of "either as the thing proposed, which is called *skopon,* or the attainment of the thing proposed, which is called *telos*" (205). For rhetoric the end is in the doing of rhetoric, *ho skopos,* in discovering the means of persuasion, not in the actual attainment of persuasion, for that may not be possible.

What distinguishes rhetoric from other arts that seek to persuade is that rhetoric desires to persuade everyone by means of generally held opinions and probabilities, whereas other arts or sciences are aimed at experts who know the terminology and principles of a discipline—astronomers attempt to persuade other astronomers through techniques proper to their sciences. In contrast, rhetoric's sources are probabilities and generally held opinions. On this account not all persuasion is rhetorical, only a particular kind. Riccobono notes in passing the fact that although rhetoric most often argues issues of political, judicial, and demonstrative nature, it is applicable to any matter that comes before the public, including larger matters, even scientific issues, if they are treated "in a way that is appropriate for common understanding" (205). While rhetoric shares argument with dialectics as a means of persuasion, unlike dialectics it may also call upon emotional and ethical proofs (205).

Having determined the end of rhetoric, Riccobono turns to its proper function and finds it in what he has already noted: its function is to find what would seem to persuade, the "persuasible" (Gr. *peri ekason,* Lat. *persuasibile*), as he terms it. Against Quintilian, who thought Aristotle looked only to invention for that purpose, Riccobono argues that Aristotle surely meant to include the remaining parts of the art he describes—arrangement, style, delivery—as lending themselves to persuasion. Style, for him, was not an accidental part of rhetoric but rather an integral element. He cites Franciscus Robortellus, Petrus Victorius, and M. Antonius Mairagius, and even Augustinus Valerius the Bishop of Verona, all of whom agree on this point (206).[8] In this respect, rhetoric differs greatly from its sister art, for style is not an integral part of dialectics.

Turning next to the subject matter of rhetoric, Riccobono explains that in this matter Aristotle is difficult to interpret. At one point he says that the aim of rhetoric is to find what is persuasible, at another, that it concerns matters under consideration by the body politic for which there is no art (209). He cites the disagreement of Cicero and Quintilian on the matter, the former holding that civic matters is its province, the other that all questions fall under it. Riccobono states that most informed commentators think that *peri ekason* referred not to any matter but to those pertaining to "human actions," which are included in the three kinds of rhetoric, namely, deliberative, forensic, and epideictic. He cites "the illustrious Count Jacobus Zabarella," a renowned philosopher at the University of Padua, who has written that " 'Rhetoric looks to action, not to knowledge' " and has added that " 'a person is said to be persuaded when he is convinced and wishes to act accordingly.' "9 Riccobono amplifies the point, explaining that human action is the goal whether "one persuades the citizen about those things that are suitable and right for the republic, or persuades judges, that they make judgments justly, or, by praising the good, one induces others to imitate them" (210). The concept of rhetoric as an art whose primary purpose is to achieve political action is thus an important factor that distinguishes it from dialectics, according to these Renaissance scholars.

Aristotle does not restrict rhetoric to the three varieties, however, as Riccobono points out. He says that rhetoric is applicable to any of the arts and sciences provided these are treated in a rhetorical way; but again, following Aristotle, he observes that the more an orator or a dialectician draws upon the knowledge of the sciences the more he slips into the science itself and leaves the realm of rhetoric or dialectics (211). Riccobono implies that if a rhetorician is knowledgeable he may use the terminology and principles of the sciences licitly and address its elite audience. The danger is that he may seek to gain a desired outcome by introducing proofs other than logical ones into the province of a science. For instance, he may attempt to use emotional persuasion to convince an audience of physicians to bar another physician from practice when scientific evidence should be preferred.

Riccobono next comes to the mode of consideration appropriate to rhetoric and again distinguishes this from dialectics. He first notes that rhetoric shares the airing first of general questions with dialectics and then of public questions with politics. Rhetoric, however, concerns itself with the persuasible, whereas dialectics considers the probable, and politics looks at civil matters in order to gain well-being for the populace. Zabarella, Riccobono says, agrees with him on this and points out that rhetoric effects its persuasion in three ways, " 'by arguments, by ethical speech, and by arousing the emotions' "(213). The addition of *ethos* and *pathos* is what creates the persuasible. Dialectics, then, is concerned with the probable and rhetoric with the persuasible.

This difference between the simply probable and the persuasible he thinks is an important one. But it is not recognized by all, Riccobono observes, and this creates difficulties. To resolve these he employs a minidisputation, first taking up what he perceives to be Aristotle's view and then turning to refute arguments against it. We will simply consider what he says of Aristotle's view.

> In the *Topics* Aristotle explains that probables are: "first, what is approved *by all,* for example, that good is to be sought, and also health, wealth, and life . . .; then what is approved *by many,* namely that wisdom is preferable to riches, that the soul is more important than the body, and that the gods exist; then, what is approved *by all the wise,* namely that the goods of the soul are better than the goods of the body, that from nothing nothing comes and that the virtues are good; then, what is approved *by most of the wise,* that virtue is to be sought for its own sake, that no body is without parts, that there are not infinite worlds; then, what is approved *by the most outstanding among the wise,* namely, that the soul is eternal, that there is a fifth essence; and finally, things that are *repugnant to the opinions of many,* even though they are approved *by some who are very wise.*" (214)

I have italicized the source of the opinions. These furnish the ground of propositions for dialectics.

Riccobono next remarks that in the *Rhetoric* Aristotle teaches that rhetoric does not come to conclusions on matters by reasoning with tight syllogisms or from what is concluded by true syllogisms. It is concerned merely with persuasibles. A persuasible is "the acknowledged probable [*probabile confessum*], that is, not the probable in an absolute sense [*probabile simpliciter*], but a kind that might even be approved by some who are very wise, and especially the probable of the type that either all or many assent to" (215). Riccobono goes on to say that "the persuasible is not everything that is probable but definite things that appear that way to all or to many" (215). It is what can be expected to persuade (247).

Riccobono then reviews what he has established. First is "that the persuasible differs from the probable in the same way as a species differs from a genus." A second difference is "that the probable is found only in argumentation [*logos*], whereas the persuasible is drawn also from character [*ethos*] and the emotions [*pathos*]." A third, "that the probable pertains to opinion, the persuasible to belief and persuasion." "[O]pinion," he says "is more universal than belief and persuasion, so that the former seems to pertain to dialectics, the latter to rhetoric." A fourth difference is also articulated: "that the probable is more argued than stated, the persuasible more stated than argued." The probable takes the form of question and answer; that is, one poses the matter and the other answers, while the persuasible is delivered in connected, continuous discourse (218–19).

In his development of the third point, Riccobono is less than patently clear. Aristotle would seem to have meant that the probabilities argued by rhetorical reasoning are often less strongly evidenced than are those of dialectics. This is why the appeals to emotion and from character are useful and sometimes necessary to persuade. Moreover, Aristotle implies that rhetoric's issues are those in which the common man has a deep interest and concern, and that these naturally involve the emotions.[10] Riccobono does not stress these points. The basis of his third distinction hinges on the audience's belief about finite issues: While the probable is what is held by all, by the wisest, or by some of the wise on general issues, the persuasible is what people in general believe on a particular point, and, he would probably agree, at a particular time. The only difference here seems to be the particularity of the persuasible, which he earlier said was too limited a view of rhetorical issues. Nevertheless, the point logically follows from the conception of rhetoric's scope as that of public issues, which are themselves finite. The other conclusions about the persuasible do get at aspects of rhetorical reasoning in an incisive way. The second conclusion, especially, brings out one of these in focusing on the two additional proofs of rhetoric. This would seem to be the critical difference and what makes its proofs persuasible.

Whether Riccobono invented the term *persuasible* is not clear. It is not a common term, but it does appear, interestingly enough, in Galileo's preface to his *Dialogue Concerning the Two Chief World Systems,* which may indicate that the scientist was familiar with his one-time colleague's work. The translator of the *Dialogue* was himself not acquainted with the term and renders Galileo's "ho giudicato palesare quelle probabilita che lo renderebbero persuasibile, dato che la Terra si movesse" (*Opere* 7: 30.21–22) as "I have thought it good to reveal those probabilities which might render this plausible, given that the earth moves" (Drake 6). In light of the rhetorical dimensions of the work, "persuasible" would have been more apt than "plausible" in this translation.

What strikes one in the literature of rhetoric today is how much Riccobono's treatment of the persuasible resembles Chaim Perelman's discussion of rhetorical proof. Both are concerned with particularity and the agreement of the audience. Perelman, however, combines dialectics and rhetoric in his "New Rhetoric" and does not sustain their differences, presumably because he does not see dialectics as providing a separate method for today's form of practical reasoning (4–9).

Riccobono has helped to clarify several difficult passages in the text of Aristotle's *Rhetoric,* especially those related to rhetoric's similarity to dialectics. What is less clear in his exposition is the nature of dialectics itself, but Riccobono's focus is on rhetoric and not dialectics. He says that a detailed knowledge of logic is not necessary for rhetoric, but only what is helpful to understand logical reasoning (246–47). He assumes his readers will turn to other sources should they wish a fuller explanation.

Dialectics in the Scholastic Tradition

Ludovico Carbone provides such a treatment in his summary of Aristotelian logic, *Introductio in logicam,* published in Venice in 1597. This work describes logic in general, including an analysis of the operations of the intellect and the nature of the "beings of reason" (*entia rationis*) with which logic is concerned. He begins with an exposition of modes of reasoning and the matter reasoned about, the subjects of Aristotle's *Prior and Posterior Analytics,* before proceeding to dialectics, the focus of the *Topics.* He notes that some commentators follow the Stoics and label the first part the judicative function of logic (99). In a similar fashion, they term the probable reasoning of dialectics *invention.* He finds these designations acceptable and descriptive even though they are not used explicitly by Aristotle. Carbone's discussion makes it clear that a knowledge of analytical logic is presupposed for understanding the probable reasoning of invention.

The most illuminating discussion of dialectics comes in his explanation in book five, where he takes up the probable or dialectical syllogism and the use of the topics in finding middle terms. Speaking of the kinds of propositions characteristic of the dialectical syllogism, Carbone mentions that these are "thought to be probable because they appear to be verisimilar and worthy of acceptance, that is, can be regarded as true" (170). He follows the text of the Topics quoted by Riccobono, noting that probable opinion means acceptance of opinions by all, or the wise—or the wisest, that is—informed opinion. Thus, opinion does not have today's connotation of idiosyncratic "personal" opinion or prejudice, as found in statements such as "everybody has a right to his or her own opinion."

Carbone states that "included among probables are those propositions that can be deduced from probables" (171). Dialectical syllogisms may also include a necessary proposition—one that is accepted as certain. Some call the dialectical syllogism an *epicherema* or an *aggressio,* he remarks, because it is so useful in "attacking an adversary" (171).

Next, Carbone explains the usefulness of the topics:

> Since human teaching makes use of opinion no less than it does of science [science denoted certain knowledge in Carbone's day], and since many more things are held by opinion than are held by science, those who wish to be concerned with the knowledge of things should be well informed about topical "places" or probable arguments. For this reason we intend in this part of our

instruction to treat it a bit more fully, though not to the full extent that is certainly possible. What motivates us to do so is the great utility beginners can gain in argumentation from knowledge of topics. This part is generally skipped in the schools, either because it is thought to be separate from logic, as indeed it is, or because it is thought to be easy and not very necessary. In my judgment, however, nothing is more suitable for an educated man than to be prepared with the benefit of this doctrine to argue knowledgeably and to persuade subtly on either side of a proposed topic, as we have taught more fully elsewhere. (173)

What motivates Carbone to give such prominence to the topics here and in the earlier lengthy treatment to which he alludes, *De oratoria, et dialectica inventione,* is the lack of interest in dialectical argument shown by many of the Humanists. The decline followed the esoteric debates on metaphysics and theology and the formulaic teaching of the late Middle Ages. Those who had the benefit of training in the art, Carbone among them, knew that such knowledge and skill had once more become very important in everyday life. Issues in which the public had an interest and a stake were being debated increasingly as the Protestant Reformation and the Scientific Revolution evolved. No longer were debates simply school exercises. The Collegio Romano was particularly noteworthy for its preservation of the best of scholastic training, combining it with the more popular *studia humanitatis.*[11]

Carbone's summary of the workings of the middle term of the syllogism in science and in dialectics illuminates by its brevity and clarity. (The middle term is, of course, the part of the major and minor premises that permits one to move from the premises to the conclusion. In the example "*white* reflects light; snow is *white;* therefore, snow reflects light," "white" is the middle term that permits one to draw the conclusion.) Carbone's explanation is worth quoting in full.

A dialectical middle, or argument, is something probable invented to induce belief; it is conjoined verisimilarly either to both extremes of a question or to one or the other so as to gain an assent to what is to be proved, though without absolute necessity.

In this the dialectical argument differs from the demonstrative, since the latter is joined to its extremes necessarily and thus generates a perfect and indubitable conclusion; the former is regarded as cohering only probably. On this account it happens that the demonstrative argument can become a dialectical argument if one does not advert to its necessity, for anything that is necessary can be regarded as probable in the judgment of the many. Hence it is that the teaching on the invention of the dialectical middle can also serve for discovering necessary middles. For that reason, when treating of the invention of the demonstrative middle [i.e., that of scientific reasoning] in the second book of the *Posterior Analytics,* Aristotle refers back to the teaching contained in the *Topics.* In the books of the latter he occasionally mentions that the treatment of topics is common to both the dialectician and the philosopher, that is, to the person arguing probably and to the person arguing demonstratively. (173)

The topics, then, can be used in finding what is likely to be true based not on certain reasoning but on what is only probably so.

By extension, we can see how the topics can also serve the needs of exposition when one is describing what is the case. For example, should we wish to describe the effects of water pollution on fish and other wildlife, we would invoke the middle term, the chemical cause, linking it to its likely deleterius effects.[12]

Further, it follows from the discussions of these two Renaissance expositors of Aristotelian teaching, a proper "dialectical" exposition would differ from a persuasible or rhetorical one by keeping *ethos* and *pathos* out of the discourse as much as possible.

Carbone goes on to show the relation of the topics to the middle term of the probable syllogism.

This argument or middle term is commonly named using the translation of the Greek *topos* or the Latin *locus,* and the books that treat of the invention of topics are called the *Topics* or in Latin, the *Places,* although "place" designates the argument itself more than the seat of the argument or where the argument may be found. On this account a topic is generally defined as the seat of an argument or the place from which it can be obtained, for when topics are known arguments are easily discovered. Aristotle spoke of this not only as a place but metaphorically as an element, because, although simple, it becomes the origin of many arguments. (173–74)

In this way, Carbone clarifies the difference between the "topic" as the more dynamic instrument for creating an argument and the setpiece or pat line of development of the "place." The one is a heuristic device, the other a filler from a storehouse of commonplaces.

Taking his cue from Cicero, Boethius, and Agricola, Carbone mentions two kinds of dialectical topics: *intrinsic* and *extrinsic*.[13] He says that among intrinsic topics are three varieties: "the thing from which the argument is sought or things that are conjoined with it or those that are disjoined from it." The topics of definition, description, and etymology are examples of the first variety; wholes, parts, causes, effects, antecedents, or consequents are examples of the second; while the third includes the topics of similars, greater, lesser, equals, dissimilars, opposites, and repugnants. Extrinsic topics like Aristotle's inartistic proofs have been enumerated in great number, he says, but he suggests that for dialectics the one of importance is authority (176–77).

Carbone further points out that two applications of the topics are possible: the one common, "when it is considered generally and not as applied to a particular subject matter, the other proper, when accommodated to a determinate matter of a particular art, as when the topic of definition is confined to nature, to morality, to rhetoric, or to any other art. For each art and science has its own proper principles that are not applicable to another discipline." (176). He notes in this context that the major and proper topics of dialectics are genus, definition, property, and accident. Others are various amplifications of these, such as those mentioned above. *Genus* has retained its meaning, but the other terms may not be as obvious to modern readers. By *definition* is meant the distinguishing characteristics, or the differentia that sets aside a species from other species; this is sometimes called *species* or *differentiae* instead of definition. *Property* means what is intrinsically bound up with the nature of the thing being considered, such as trunks in regard to trees, whereas *accident* is something that may or may not be part of it, such as needles or leaves. The proper topics of dialectic become common when used to develop general matters in any investigation.

In the text that follows, Carbone describes each of the common dialectical topics and gives examples of how arguments might be developed from them. There is not space to summarize these, but modern versions are to be found in Edward P.J. Corbett's *Classical Rhetoric for the Modern Student* (94–132) and Winifred Bryan Horner's *Rhetoric in the Classical Tradition* (chs. 4–5).

Carbone offers a series of animadversions near the end of the text that further clarify the practice of dialectics. He first urges that the student study the topics carefully and practice using them so that they are "placed before his very eyes," with the result that he will not need to recall rules but simply apply them "spontaneously" (206). Overuse also has its dangers, he notes, and cautions that "we should beware lest out of vain contentiousness we attempt to draw arguments from any topic whatever for proving any question whatever, since not every topic will be suitable to proving it; for not everything has causes, parts, opposites, etc., that can offer a topic or source for arguments" (206).

The "proper" or special topics also receive attention from Carbone. He explains how a student goes about acquiring knowledge of these for a discipline:

> First he should learn the proper meanings of ambiguous words and terms of that art; then he should perceive the first principles on which the entire teaching depends. After that he should learn the subject matter universally, the parts, causes, and properties; after that he should go to the species. He should do this in physics, metaphysics, and ethics, and in other arts and in all of learning. Thus only the person who has filled his mind with the doctrine of common and proper topics can be called a true dialectician. (207)

Aristotle offered advice in the eighth book of the *Topics* for developing an argument and for conducting debate. These notes guided the development of the disputation, the academic form of dialectics popular in the Middle Ages and practiced well into the nineteenth century. The question-and-answer structure furnished the underlying conception of the disputation, but it also permitted the speaker or writer to develop a continuous flow of discourse (which would often be published), uninterrupted by interrogation from the respondent.[14] Instead, the author posed the question, treated the positions an opponent might be expected to give, and refuted or acknowledged each part of these. He then presented his own position in light of the opposition. Likewise, the author of a treatise on a serious subject would be expected to bear in mind the basic structure of disputation. He would air opposing views but in this case in an expository fashion.

Not surprisingly, then, Carbone offers guidance for the development and organization of expository discourse:

> [W]hen any entire matter is to be explained by us, it is usually correct to proceed in this order: treating of the name, existence, nature, and cause on account of which it is; its effect or function; its parts, species, similars, and contraries. Or, the whole treatise might be reduced to the four questions: is it, what is it, what kind is it, and why is it [of this kind]. If we are to treat of some virtue, its necessity or desirability should be demonstrated, its object and its subject, from which its nature will be made apparent; then its conditions and properties, the ways in which it may be compared, and in what way impediments to it may be removed. (210)

A different pattern is advised for confutation.

> First, the truth should be confirmed, and from the truth the errors of others should be refuted; second, the opinions of others should first be referred to and refuted, and afterwards what is to be held should be stated; third, the arguments in favor of each side should first be advanced, along with opinions, and then the truth should be explained and proved, and lastly arguments to the contrary should be refuted. (210)

He remarks that "[p]ractically all schools now follow this order, and Aristotle approves it at the beginning of the third book of the *Metaphysics.*" Near the end of these words of advice he cautions his readers not to take them too slavishly.

> [W]hat we have said about the methods to be followed in arguing or in writing are not to be taken as sacred rules; rather, when the circumstances of the matter we are treating persuade otherwise, it is all right to depart reasonably from the prescribed formulas. What should also move us in so doing is the fear that by always following the same path we may fall into a type of complacency and fastidiousness. (210)

Carbone completes his discussion of logic with an explanation of sophistic syllogisms.

Modern Applications of Renaissance Concepts

From these two texts the modern teacher of rhetoric and composition can gain insight into how strongly the aims of inquiry and discourse influenced the nature of the disciplines of rhetoric and dialectics in centuries past. James Kinneavy's *A Theory of Discourse* makes a convincing argument that this is still a useful principle that enables us to distinguish genres. He finds that such aims undergird the thought of both ancient and modern theorists.[15] Should we adopt the approaches of these two Renaissance texts, the following principles would dominate our teaching of rhetoric and composition.

The acknowledged aim of rhetoric would be to persuade. The aim of modern dialectical discourse—scientific and informative writing—would remain what it was for the ancients: to discern what is true or seems to be true. The invention of arguments or material in each of these genres would be governed by the aims. In view of rhetoric's aim, rhetorical topics would be used to select logical, ethical, and emotional appeals that would sway an audience. Given that aim, an examination of the political or social ends sought by the writer would also become an appropriate element of the rhetorical process. Ethical considerations would thus be integral to "the composing process." Authors would likewise need to analyze audiences to determine what would probably move them to action or persuade them to revise their thinking. Presumably that audience would be a popular audience.

For teachers who have followed the path recommended by Corbett and Horner in the teaching of composition, the rhetorical principles just noted are surely familiar and unremarkable. The narrowing of rhetoric's scope and the insertion of the dialectical dimension, on the other hand, are far more problematic. The conception of the two as separate arts seems to offer the advantage of providing a clearer view of what is not rhetorical. In treating subjects where knowledge is accepted as the principal aim, dialectical probing and reasoning about what seems most probable would hold out the hope of a resolution to general questions, or, in the case of informative writing, it would ensure an airing of the reasons something seems most probably true. The dialectical topics of definition, species, property, and accident—along with modern additions such as the tagmemic grid and the pentad—would serve the purposes not only of dialectical argumentation but of exposition in helping students lay out what appear to be the causes, the effects, the natures of their subjects. Writers would be led to assess issues from either side more fully, exposing all the relevant points to provide a clearer picture of the best alternative explanation. The range of opinion on an issue, including the context in which certain views are held, could be thoroughly aired and primary values assigned according to the reigning opinions of the day. In this way writers might remain comparatively "objective" and not be tempted to slight either evidence or opposing positions because a subjective view is all that can be expected.

For Renaissance teachers of rhetoric, the distinctive aims of rhetoric and dialectic were stressed because the scholarly community expected them to be followed. Although in practice dialecticians might use rhetorical devices to clarify, and rhetoric might employ dialectical topics and reasoning to arrive at solutions to dilemmas, the dialectician would not be respected should he rest his case on emotional arguments, nor would the rhetorician be heeded if he persisted in prolonged eristic determinations. One wonders if we do not make these same evaluations of arguments when we stop and think critically, even though the discriminate terminology has disappeared from our teaching.

Notes

1. Ong discusses dialectic in the Middle Ages and the Renaissance in chapter 4 and the effect of Ramus's reforms in chapters 8 and 9. Enrico Berti provides an excellent analysis of the various usages of the art as the Greeks conceived of it. See also Howell's treatment of the Continental scene before he turns to England.

2. Kathleen Welch has carefully analyzed our "appropriation" of classical rhetoric and summarized the reactions of some critics of the ancient art in part 1.

3. Carbone's writings are detailed in my essay "The Rhetoric Course at the Collegio Romano in the Latter Half of the Sixteenth Century," n. 21.

4. Riccobono taught at Padua from 1571 until shortly before his death in 1599. My colleague William A. Wallace has made his unpublished translation of Riccobono's commentary on Aristotle's *Rhetoric* available to me. I have edited this, comparing it to the original text. All citations are to the 1579 work.

5. Carbone's work on logic has been translated in part by Professor Wallace. I have used his translation, citing the original in the text. Wallace points out parallels between Carbone's book and Galileo's manuscript on logic in his introduction to *Tractatio* (lxiii–lxxi).

6. One of Riccobono's letters to Galileo will be found in *Opere,* 10:30.

7. Cranz lists ten Latin translations, one Italian vernacular and nine commentaries published in the sixteenth century (220–21). Charles Lohr provides brief biographical notes for authors of these editions.

8. Franciscus Robortellus was born in Utine in 1516 and died in 1567. A well-known classicist and rhetorician, he taught at Pisa in the 1540s and in Padua in the next decade. He authored a number of books on rhetoric and poetics. Petrus Victorius was born in Florence in 1499 and died there in 1585; he was also a classicist and a professor of moral philosophy. M. Antonius Maioragius, born in 1514, studied rhetoric and mathematics at Milan and taught rhetoric there; he died in 1555. These biographical notes are based on Lohr's accounts.

9. Giacomo Zabarella, born in Padua in 1533, studied humanities under Franciscus Robortellus and logic under Bernardinus Tomi-

tanus. A very influential philosopher and logician, Zabarella died in 1589.

10. Larry Arnhart makes the point that the enthymeme, the heart of rhetorical argument in Aristotle's *Rhetoric,* is distinctive because it appeals to the emotions as well as to the intellect (40–41).

11. I describe the curriculum at the Roman College in "The Rhetoric Course."

12. William A. Wallace notes the relevance of the topics for both exposition and argument and gives many examples of their application in "Aitia" (107–34).

13. Carbone outlines the treatment given by each of these authors in *On oratoria,* book I, chapter 16; for Boethius see Stump; for a summary of the topical tradition see Green-Pedersen.

14. A discussion of the structure of question-and-answer underlying disputations, letters, and treatises of the Renaissance will be found in my "Dialectic and Rhetoric."

15. Kinneavy analyzes the principles of division of the aims of discourse in schools of thought from Aristotle through Jakobson, chapter 2, especially figure II, 2, 65.

Works Cited

Arnhart, Larry. *Aristotle on Political Reasoning: A Commentary On the "Rhetoric."* DeKalb: Northern Illinois UP, 1981.

Berti, Enrico. "Ancient Greek Dialectic as Expression of Freedom of Thought and Speech." *Journal of the History of Ideas* 39 (1978): 347–70.

Carbone, Ludovico. *De oratoria, et dialectica inventione, vel de locis communibus.* Venice, 1589.

———. *Introductio in logicam.* Venice, 1597.

Corbett, Edward P.J. *Classical Rhetoric for the Modern Student.* 3rd ed. Oxford: Oxford UP, 1990.

Cranz, F. Edward. *A Bibliography of Aristotle Editions: 1501–1600.* 2d ed. Addenda and rev. Charles B. Schmitt. Bibliotheca Bibliographica Aureliana, XXXVIII*. Baden-Baden: Verlag Valentin Koerner, 1984.

Drake, Stillman. *Galileo, Dialogue Concerning the Two Chief World Systems.* Berkeley: U of California P, 1962.

Galilei, Galileo. *Le Opere di Galileo Galilei.* Ed. Antonio Favaro, 20 vols. in 21. Florence: G. Barbera, 1890–1900. rpt. 1968.

———. *Tractatio de Praecognitionibus et praecognitis and Tractatio de demonstratione.* Trans. William F. Edwards. Intro. and commentary William A. Wallace. Padua: Antenore, 1988.

Green-Pedersen, Niels J. *The Tradition of the Topics in the Middle Ages.* Munich-Vienna: Philosophia Verlag, 1984.

Gross, Alan G. *The Rhetoric of Science.* Cambridge: Harvard UP, 1990.

Horner, Winifred Bryan. *Rhetoric in the Classical Tradition.* New York: St. Martin's, 1988.

Howell, Wilbur S. *Logic and Rhetoric in England, 1500–1700.* Princeton: Princeton UP, 1956.

Kinneavy, James L. *A Theory of Discourse.* New York: Norton, 1980.

Lohr, Charles H. *Latin Aristotle Commentaries-II Renaissance Authors.* Florence: Leo S. Olschki, 1988.

Moss, Jean Dietz. "Dialectic and Rhetoric: Questions and Answers in the Copernican Revolution." *Argumentation* 5 (1991): 17–37.

――――. "The Rhetoric Course at the Collegio Romano In the Latter Half of the Sixteenth Century." *Rhetorica* 4:2 (1986): 137–51.

Nelson, John S., Allan Megill, and Donald N. McCloskey. *The Rhetoric of the Human Sciences.* Madison: U of Wisconsin P, 1987.

Ong, Walter J. *Ramus: Method and the Decay of Dialogue.* Cambridge: Harvard UP, 1958.

Perelman, Chaim, and L. Olbrechts-Tyteca. *The New Rhetoric: A Treatise on Argumentation.* Notre Dame: U of Notre Dame P, 1969.

Riccobono, Antonio. *Aristotelis Ars Rhetorica.* Venice, 1579. Robortellus, Franciscus. *De artificio dicendi.* Bologna, 1567.

――――. *In librum Aristotelis De arte poetica explicationes.* Florence, 1548.

Stump, Eleonore, ed. and trans. *Boethius's De Topicis Differentis.* Ithaca: Cornell UP, 1978.

Wallace, William A. "*Aitia:* Causal Reasoning in Composition and Rhetoric." *Rhetoric and Praxis: The Contribution of Classical Rhetoric to Practical Reasoning.* Ed. J. D. Moss. Washington, DC: The Catholic U of America P, 1985.

Welch, Kathleen E. *The Contemporary Reception of Classical Rhetoric: Appropriations of Ancient Discourse.* Hillsdale, NJ: Lawrence Erlbaum, 1990.

Dialectic/
Rhetoric/
Writing

Kathleen E. Welch

Writing is dialectic. It is dialectic in Plato's sense of a strategy of attaining knowledge through the action of the soul and through the action of language. Writing is also dialectic in the generic sense of a productive clash, a tension of competing interests. Good writing always derives from the interaction of this dialectical clash, this struggle for creation through weaving disparate strands. An analogy between dialectic and weaving is chosen by Plato in *Cratylus* to establish language interaction and mutual dependence (Cornford 246).

I want to explore ways we can use the dialectic that is inherent in writing to structure writing classes, a strategy that recognizes the reality of dialectical clashes. Dialectic that forms all parts of the writing course works to persuade students to interiorize these dissonances, i.e., it becomes a rhetoric. Resistance to writing—both by the students and by the instructor—is not overcome but is, like Plato's construction of the competing dark horse and light horse in *Phaedrus*—harnessed for productive use. So the aspects of writing that are regarded as problems to be solved are transformed into productive contraries that are embraced. This view of writing grounds itself in a holistic view of discourse close to Hegel's, not a materialistic one.[1]

It is important to establish here that by dialectic I do not mean formal logic, or the use of propositions and statements. Beginning with Aristotle, especially in the *Topics,* dialectic came to mean formal logic. By the Middle Ages, dialectic was part of the trivium and usually indicated formal logic.

Whately in the early nineteenth century relied on this use, and much of the work in argumentation in today's writing texts derives from this nineteenth-century incarnation of dialectic. The empirical, rationalist background is revealed in the linearity of this kind of dialectic. It is common now to translate the logic of the medieval trivium with the word *dialectic*. The meanings, in Aristotle and in medieval writing and pedagogy, are not the meanings Plato developed. He sees dialectic as an investigation of the Forms, including the ways that the Forms combine and divide to create "reality." *Interaction* is the key term. Propositional statements are not the issue. Gadamer's rereading of Hegel by connecting him with the organic language theory of ancient philosophy is a recognition of this same issue: Dialectic in the Platonic sense is motion, the discovery of a oneness in multiplicity, and the interaction of Forms.

The propositional sense of Aristotle's and medieval thinkers' dialectic is in fact counterproductive in the writing classroom. The main reason for this is the putting aside of psychological issues. The whole mind of the writer is not used.

Since I am relying on the Platonic construction of dialectic, I do not use the idea that dialectic is a mere pairing of binary opposites. Rather, this Platonic dialectic for the classroom is the movement forward to new insight from the pairing of oppositional forces. This dialectic derives its energy from the making of connections.

I propose here setting up three familiar pedagogical techniques in a manner that forms dialectic in the writing class. These teaching devices can be combined in new ways to form valuable writing knowledge for student/writers and the instructor/writer. These techniques are: (1) the writing workshop as dialectic, an arena in which all the gathered writers continuously interact in speaking and writing; (2) the use of critics' sheets, or particular, written strategies for recasting, to generate multiple drafts of a piece of writing and to compel shifting perspectives toward the text; and (3) the teacher/student dialogue on paper. These devices can be combined to promote a shift in ordinary writerly thinking in two ways. First, the logic-chopping (or pseudo-logic-chopping) pedagogy of the current-traditional paradigm is transcended through the repeated questioning of the writer's motive.[2] Second, the less familiar pedagogical limitation of so-called process writing instruction is overcome by maintaining criteria that all the writers in the class understand.

These uses of dialectics in the writing class deny by their very nature the static texts that dominate many writing courses. Instead of stasis, dialectics require text fluidity. Because of the workshop construction and the requirement for continual text production, stasis is hard to achieve. The teaching of writing acquired this static model, with reification as its epistemology, from the discipline of English, which is the source of the anointment of particular texts into a stable body of works and the unself-conscious interpretation of those texts. I want to turn for a moment to the stasis of the discipline of English and how its traditional study of a fixed and arbitrary body of texts has provided a structural basis for the nondialectical teaching of writing. The static model has defined literary studies for the last two generations since T. S. Eliot and F. R. Leavis canonized particular texts and made the discipline of English more respectable than the previous Great Man approach had been able to do.[3] It is this creation of an unchanging collection of great art that creates the basis for mystifying the act of writing, whether by so-called great writers or by students and their teachers. Great writing has been limping along with the ball and chain of religious fervor attached to it. Religious objects are by their nature stable and unchanging. When a literary text is canonized, its divinity prevents any exploration of its essential flux and life.

These companion problems from the discipline of English—a concept of great literary artifacts that resemble antiques and the attendant worship of that art—have provided the foundation of much of the teaching of writing. Religiosity is even more disastrous in writing pedagogy than in literature pedagogy because of the emphasis on the textual artifact, on the very last conceptualization of a piece of writing. Writing pedagogy requires a careful working out of all the tension that precedes a "final" version. In other words, much of the teaching of writing has unself-consciously formed itself after the static model of old-fashioned literary studies, with a canon to be revered and a language world divorced from all ordinary language use. The struggle against this reified material has been one of the explosive sources of interest in composition, as well as in contemporary literary theory, including deconstruction. The work against the current-traditional paradigm, which exists only because of the stasis that defines the formulaic, is an excellent example of the movement in composition and rhetoric to discard worn-out traditional literary epistemologies. The serious study of noncanonical student texts is another example. But because we are working against largely unconscious motives (again, based on a faith in literature, or "English," that is religious) we need to examine vigorously the philosophical bases of our work. Static writing pedagogy remains firmly fixed in many classrooms. More seriously, so-called process writing pedagogy has often become equally static, as a glance at each year's crop of freshman writing texts indicates.

Deriving from the canonical, reified, and mystified traditional teaching of literature, static writing pedagogy creates its own unique stasis: the writing textbook. Aside from the hardening of the categories of the prescriptive formulas that make these books, the student writer is made to be ahistorical, deriving from no culture, and therefore having no values. Richard Ohmann, in *English in America,* describes it like this: "The student . . . is defined only by studenthood, not by any other attributes. He is classless, sexless though generically male, timeless" (145). The student writer in these texts, which generate enormous revenues, cannot possibly engage in the dialectic that is writing. Rather, by steeping in the blandness of stasis, student writers come to hate writing and so lose part of their potential ability for thinking. Only by denying this familiar stasis that instructors and students are invited to acquire, by recognizing fluidity in written discourse, are we able to recast writing. Dialectic offers us a way to transcend stasis. It is not boring.

The main characteristic of this crucial fluidity, and of classical and modern conceptions of dialectic, is a constant resistance to closure. Maintaining the idea that all language is a kind of flux reveals writing possibilities to students and to instructors, who engage in dialectics with their students.

Let us apply the idea of dialectic's nonclosure to the three standard techniques I have offered in the workshop, the metacommentary on student texts, and the use of critics' sheets. When student writers become readers in the writing workshop, they prod, question, and essentially offer new streams of invention to the writer whose text is the center of attention. This pedagogical strategy, which comes from the mode of so-called creative writing classes, a phrase that is redundant, concentrates all critical energy on one student's text, provides her with an outpouring of possibilities that can be accepted or rejected, according to the writer's judgment, and supplies an interaction that sends the writer back to the text even while it may be uncomfortable. This discomfort and clash of opinions generated by the concentration on one writer's text also allow spoken clashes to occur. Looking at a student's writing as seriously as one might look at Shakespeare in another class or Roland Barthes in another and using some of the same approaches but dropping the mystified fervor provides the momentum for the writing workshop.

The workshop, relying on the persuasive force of the writers who gather together, compels the writer to shift stance, or at least to consider the possibility of such a shift. This internal dialectic, this clash of conflicting strands in the writer and in the readers, breaks down monolithic tendencies of many student writers trained so well in the belief that good writing just springs out, perfectly formed, lovely to behold. For example, student writers are often wedded to one voice (usually a school-writing voice), one style, one *ethos*. The workshop dialectic persuades the writer through collaboration that other possibilities exist. In other words, any closure that the writer may have felt is exploded by the rest of the class. The harnessed contraries interact and drive the writer forward to new knowledge. Nonclosure means the promotion of fluidity, the enhanced capacity to revise the writing, and the resistance of stasis.

Critics' sheets, my term for what other people have called revision guides, work within the larger dialectic of the writing workshop. These texts, written by the instructor, set up avenues of continuous response for the workshop, including the writer who now becomes a critic. They prevent closure. I borrow here Kenneth Burke's conception of the critic. In *Permanence and*

Change, Burke asserts that all living beings are critics, even chickens who respond to bells that signal food is available (5). The bell response here becomes a critical act. It is a response to a particular context. The chicken experiences desire triggered by the sound and it seeks to fulfill that desire. Criticism for Burke then has to do with the creation of appetite. Burke's idea that the act of criticism is a complex, instinctive act that requires more than the conscious mind is the one I want to use here. The names "revision guide" or "questions for study," are fine as far as they go, but they do not take into account enough of the human psyche that produces the writing. These phrases bypass the unconscious. I want to follow Burke and embrace the unconscious as a primary aspect of writing. The critics in critics' sheets are invited, because of the instinctual nature of the critical act, to look for the creation of an appetite in decoders and the possibilities for feeding it. One example of a dialectic set up in the critics' sheets is the questions for identifying the *ethos* of the writer. Searching—largely subtextually—the nature of the character of the writer, for the way that belief is engendered by a particular manipulation of written discourse, shows the workshop the gap between the intentionality of the writer and the execution of the intention residing in the text. When more than one student critic discovers a writing issue like this, its persuasiveness for the writer is deeply felt. A dialectic is interiorized. If disagreement among the critics develops over the *ethos,* that very disagreement forces the writer to depend on her own writing judgment, to decide what she thinks of her text. The key is that the writer, in the midst of the workshop dialectic, is compelled to respond actively. Since her work provides the course text at the time, she must remain active. The dialectic here resides in the pairing of oppositional views—the student essay and the critics' sheet harnessed in search of a more effective essay. Neither one is right, since writing does not conform to the definiteness of good or evil. But the probing of the essay through this dialectic leads to collaborative search for effective choices. The critics' sheet, then, sets in motion a probing of the essay, a dialectical inquiry. The dialectical writing class allows students to see the priests of the canon perform a task no different from that of the students themselves. They see their teachers write. They see them struggle with the same primary issues.

Writing instructors have encouraged their status as nonwriters by linguistically perpetuating mystification and stasis and by refusing to call students what they can and should be called: critics. This denial collapses the dialectic merely by naming wrongly.

The clash of differing opinion based on the critics' sheets and on the workshops prevents closure and promotes the holistic experience of a piece of written discourse. Another way of stating this phenomenon is to say that it gives up the models of traditional literary studies, the reification of writing into a canon that becomes an object of worship.

Nonclosure is similarly available in a third dialectic that can help to energize the writing classroom, the student/instructor dialogue on paper, or the metacommentary. The pairing of oppositional issues that defines this dialectic begins with the instructor who writes a response to a student essay. In a dialectical writing class, these comments provide another text available for probing and searching. One way of setting up the dialectical pairing is to present these responses as a result of choice. The instructor reinforces writing as a series of choices, of the working out of certain beliefs, by presenting her written comments, as a product of choice. Since not all issues raised in the student essay can be treated, some aspects have been privileged. The dialectic of metacommentary advances when the student is offered the opportunity to respond to the comments in writing. These comments can be attached to the next essay and these student responses can be further commented on by the instructor. A series of texts are generated by instructor and student essentially writing to each other. This dialectic, which requires surprisingly little time, engenders a sense of possibility, one of the crucial aspects of dialectics and writing. It enables the student/writer and the instructor/writer to carry on their dialogue through the challenge of pairing oppositional forces. The language of this dialectic does not end because the material that produces a response has embedded in it the possibility of further thinking in writing. A dialectical chain of discourse is created. All parts are linked.

These student metacommentaries can consist of responses to previous instructor comments, to class discussion that relates to the writing, and to the writer's sense of change in her writing. The instructor's comments interact with the students' comments to create a potentially continuous exchange. These risk-free texts increase the student's sense of power in writing and reveals important insight to the instructor.

The three dialectics—the workshop structure, the use of critics' sheets, and the use of metacommentaries—share a crucial value. They require the use of many parts of the psyche. The search for the undiscovered, for the possible, that defines dialectic, is not confined to the linearity of the current-traditional formula or the stasis of the one-dimensional. The nonengagement of students' minds and instructors' minds—perhaps one definition of boredom—has been the unintended result of many writing classes. In these monotonal settings, writing becomes utterly linear because it depends on single-level formulas and an absence of interaction. The dialectic in writing pedagogy converts the formulaic and the linear into a clash of interests. It requires writing of many kinds and involvement by all the people in the class. The use of these dialectics leads us away from many of the complaints of writing pedagogy: boredom, too little substance, an inability to break free of the merely mechanical.

Change supplies the possibility of dialectic. Students—largely because of school training—resist change. The student judgment that her text is complete and cannot be changed dismisses any possibility of real revising. The activity of dialectic ends this passive judgment of completion. Dialectic explodes this problem through the creation of energy. The interaction and change of dialectic enable us to transcend the monotony of the formulaic.

Dialectic and its attendant nonclosure in the teaching of writing lead to yet another crucial language phenomenon in forming/thinking/writing, Ann Berthoff's formulation of what we do in the writing classroom. It explodes the idea of utopia in writing. That is, the powerful idea of a perfect text is put aside when fluidity is the primary element. Dialectics are characterized by movement. Utopias are static. In the dialectical classroom, no perfect writer will emerge at the end of the semester. A utopian scene of a writer who can produce consistently excellent prose cannot be the goal of the dialectical paradigm because it is impossible to realize, and, even more importantly, it is undesirable. Without dialectical tension— Plato's engagement of tensions—good writing is hard to achieve, and good rewriting is nearly impossible. The task for the designer of this dialectic, the writing instructor, is to form (shape) the writing class that not only recognizes the inevitable tension of writing as an action but also exploits it and embraces it, even while it is filled with difficulty.

Dialectic and writing instruction depend then on three primary issues: (1) changes in expectation of what one takes from the course, i.e., the putting aside of a utopian aim and an embracing of tension-filled struggle, both of which depend on nonclosure; (2) identification of writing energy through many kinds of interaction; and (3) the recognition of the student as an active, historical self rather than as an inert, unchanging being whose passivity defines her, the view implicitly taken by most textbook writers. Dialetic changes the usual "process" techniques by making them active.

If with dialectic we move away from the linearity that characterizes most writing texts and many writing classes, it is because in the dialectical writing class we attach a text to a human being. The text is allowed to have its encoder context. This connection is why Aristotle, in book I of the *Rhetoric,* says that *ethos* is probably the most important of the artistic proofs, or interior persuaders. The encoder who resides in a text is the part of discourse that sets up the conditions of belief for us. To continue the example of the presentation of *ethos* in a piece of writing, as one of the issues that arises in a dialectical context, we can see that this presentation has embedded in it the choices a writer has made, whether fully consciously or not. Aristotle, again in book I of the *Rhetoric,* says that "Character is manifested in choice, and choice is related to the end or aim" (Cooper 46). Dialectic is one way of making choices.

Dialectic can act as a paradigm for the teaching and learning of writing, three of its virtues being: (1) it avoids hardened categories where stasis easily takes over, as in the current-traditional paradigm; (2) it has no closure, so that there is a constant recognition of the fluidity of language; and (3) it requires continual text production.

Dialectic allows us to work out in the writing classroom a subversion of the passivity that school engenders and rewards. David Gross discussed this use of dialectic recently in *College English:* "The collective nature of the classroom enterprise can sometimes subvert the separations and fragmentations of 'normal' academic thought. The genuine interactions in classroom engagements with a common text (when they in fact occur) allow us to achieve the dialectical knowledge which most of our cultural training makes so hard for us to see" (184). Dialectic interaction in writing classes can then become a center that not only helps students write more effectively but also enables them to critique their other studies.

Dialectic, an important way of thinking available to us from classical rhetoric, is another way that theory and practice are seen to be the same thing with differing emphases. It provides energy for the teaching of writing and can be applied to all of language studies.

Notes

1. For a persuasive argument of Hegel's affinity with ancient Greek philosophy, see Hans-Georg Gadamer's "Hegel and the Dialectic of the Ancient Philosophers," in his *Hegel's Dialectic* (1–35).

2. Andrea Lunsford and Lisa Ede use the phrase "logic-chopping automaton" to describe one kind of contemporary reception of classical rhetoric. See "On Distinctions Between Classical and Contemporary Rhetoric."

3. See E. D. Hirsch, Jr., "Remarks on Composition to the Yale English Department" in *The Rhetorical Tradition and Modern Writing* and Terry Eagleton, *Literary Theory,* for two treatments.

Works Cited

Berthoff, Ann. *Forming/Thinking/Writing.* Upper Montclair, NJ: Boynton/Cook, 1980.

_____. *The Making of Meaning*. Upper Montclair, NJ: Boynton/ Cook, 1981.

Burke, Kenneth. *Permanence and Change*. 3rd ed. Berkeley: U of California P, 1984.

Cooper, Lane, trans. *The Rhetoric of Aristotle*. Englewood Cliffs, NJ: Prentice, 1932.

Cornford, Francis, trans. *Plato's Theory of Knowledge: The Theaetetus and the* Sophist *of Plato*. Indianapolis: Bobbs, 1957.

Eagleton, Terry. *Literary Theory*. Minneapolis: U of Minnesota P, 1983.

Gadamer, Hans-Georg. *Hegel's Dialectic*. Trans. P. Christopher Smith. New Haven: Yale UP, 1976.

Gross, David. "Infinite Indignation: Teaching, Dialectical Vision, and Blake's *Marriage of Heaven and Hell*." *College English* 48 (1986): 175–86.

Lunsford, Andrea A., and Lisa S. Ede. "On Distinctions Between Classical and Contemporary Rhetoric." *Essays on Classical Rhetoric and Modern Discourse*. Ed. Robert J. Connors, Lisa S. Ede, and Andrea A. Lunsford. Carbondale, IL: Southern Illinois UP, 1984.

Murphy, James J., ed. *The Rhetorical Tradition and Modern Writing*. New York: MLA, 1982.

Ohmann, Richard. *English in America*. New York: Oxford UP, 1976.

Plato. *Phaedrus*. Trans. W. C. Helmbold and W. G. Rabinowitz. Indianapolis: Bobbs, 1956.

10 Classical Rhetoric and Group Writing
A Warranted Relationship

Richard Leo Enos

> Participants in collaborative groups learn when they challenge one another with questions, when they use the evidence and information available to them, when they develop relationships among issues, when they evaluate their own thinking. In other words, they learn when they assume that knowledge is something they can help create rather than something to be received whole from someone else.
> —Anne Ruggles Gere, *Writing Groups* 69

This essay makes a single but important point, one intended to offer a positive response to the above statement of Anne Ruggles Gere by offering a system that facilitates how writing group participants may challenge each other in the manner she suggests.[1] Classical rhetoric provides heuristic procedures that, when adapted to group writing, facilitate both communication between participants and the composing process itself. Our field has well-conceived applications of classical rhetoric for contemporary composition with Edward P.J. Corbett's *Classical Rhetoric for the Modern Student* and Winifred Bryan Horner's *Rhetoric in the Classical Tradition*. Such texts and numerous articles have provided individual authors with heuristics facilitating thought and expression. The task here is to discuss the benefits of extending applications of classical rhetoric from individual authors to group writing in the hope that such a discussion will prompt composition specialists to consider the application of classical rhetoric to collaborative writing as it has been so effectively done with single authors.

Clearly, the application of classical rhetoric to group writing necessitates adjustments for markedly different writing contexts than those an individual author confronts. In group deliberation an individual's system of problem solving shifts to a constituent of a larger system, one that creates a synthetic, group rationality. Normally associated with individual writing, classical rhetoric can be modified to aid a group called into existence for the purposes of responding to or resolving a rhetorical problem. A modification of the heuristics of classical rhetoric within the context of group deliberation facilitates writing processes and the modalities of collaborative interaction. This discussion is intended to demonstrate that the potential benefits classical rhetoric offers to group writing warrant further inquiry.

Rhetorical Discourse and Group Writing

Group problem solving is similar to an individual's process because it necessitates a system, albeit an integration of the individual systems of its membership. When Noam Chomsky was concluding his review of B. F. Skinner's *Verbal Behavior,* he made the following claim: "The listener (or reader) must determine, from an exhibited utterance, what optional rules were chosen in the construction of the utterance. It must be admitted that the ability of a human being to do this far surpasses our present understanding [but] . . . any theory of learning must cope with these facts" (577). A body of research in rhetoric and composition has developed over the last twenty-five years that attempts to understand the "optional rules" by which individuals structure frameworks for the resolutions of problems. The range of inquiry growing out of this research covers the heuristics of chess playing to the mapping of decision making in artificial intelligence.

The study of rhetoric, and particularly classical theories of rhetoric, emphasizes the production and application of heuristics; rhetoric is concerned with the artificial creation of systematic procedures for generating and articulating discourse for the resolution of problematic conditions. Of equal importance, the heuristics of classical rhetoric are intended to facilitate the creation of shared meaning between rhetor and auditor (Enos and Lauer; Grimaldi). The heuristics of classical rhetoric, intended for the purpose of cocreating meaning, can be extended to share meaning not only between rhetor and auditor but also between rhetors themselves;

that is, in those writing situations that involve collaborative composing, the same heuristics that facilitate shared meaning between writer and reader can also aid in sharing meaning between plural authors. In brief, the heuristics of classical rhetoric provide a framework for structuring thought and making explicit a coherent process for inventing ideas that lead to the resolution of problems.

The advantage of applying the heuristics of rhetoric to group writing is that such heuristics provide, as Chaim Perelman and L. Olbrechts-Tyteca indicate, a "structure to establish a solidarity between accepted judgments and others which one wishes to promote" (261). Several rhetorical theories facilitate invention through heuristic procedures derived from classical rhetoric by accounting for syntactic and conceptual structuring of discourse. Rhetoricians such as Corbett (*Classical Rhetoric and the Modern Student* and "The Usefulness of Classical Rhetoric") and Perelman and Olbrechts-Tyteca (*The New Rhetoric*) have demonstrated how new theories of rhetoric can be established on classical tenets and have shown indirectly that rhetorics such as Aristotle's can use heuristic processes that can aid in articulating knowledge with others. Sometimes called "new Classicists" by Richard E. Young and others (Lunsford and Ede 113), these scholars of ancient rhetoric have sought to apply their knowledge of historical rhetoric as a theoretical basis for contemporary writing. In fact, one of the most important and dynamic topics engaging the interests of historical and contemporary rhetoricians is the implications of such relationships, as Kathleen E. Welch so thoroughly examines in her recent work, *The Contemporary Reception of Classical Rhetoric: Appropriations of Ancient Discourse.*

Most of the attention on establishing such connections between past and present focus on single authorship, that is, the nature and processes used by individual rhetors through time and across cultures. The difference is that the dynamics of group writing provide a bi- or multilateral vector to rhetoric. That is, decision making based on the heuristics of classical rhetoric provides a reciprocal interaction among participants that provides, in turn, the opportunity to have heuristics develop in a way the group believes is reasonable. In short, such groups come into existence expressly for the purpose of collaborative writing since a collective sense of rationality can be articulated. Group writing projects are rhetorical when their function is to resolve problems and secure agreement either as a means of promoting solidarity or attaining a particular goal. The benefit of rhetoric, as Frank D'Angelo indicates, is that its heuristic powers aid in facilitating the invention and articulation of argument.

In group writing the heuristics of classical rhetoric can actually help to generate systematic procedures for constructing knowledge that can be understood by others. These heuristics can be beneficial in moving a writing class from traditional methods of instruction emphasizing individual authorship to a collaborative environment, particularly in the manner described by Mary Ann Janda, since the focus of orientation shifts from the teacher to group participants whose tasks are aided by shared rhetorical systems of thought and expression ("Collaboration in a Traditional Classroom Environment" 195). In collaborative efforts, the role of the writing teachers shifts also, from the role of imparting direction to that of providing the theoretical basis upon which students can collectively create their own direction.

Collaborative and Collective Heuristics

The starting points for group writing are different from individually generated discourse, so the classical heuristics intended for single rhetors should be adapted to such differences. A group of writers engages in a rhetorical act in which members initiate deliberation with autonomous heuristic processes for structuring meaning, advancing interpretations, and establishing positions. The interaction of collaborators makes apparent both the central importance of recognizing the disparate and collective notions of knowledge and process group members bring as well as the importance of being sensitive to (and accounting for) heuristic processes involved in a synthesis of writing rationality. These heuristic presuppositions and modalities by individual group members constitute ways of constructing knowledge leading to meaning and provide strategies for articulating thoughts and sentiments. Such presuppositions in the nature and mode of expression must be synthesized since group writing is predicated on group rationality and (consequently) group agreement.

Because heuristic presumptions drive the interaction of a writing group, a clear synthesis of heuristic presumptions early in the discussion is invaluable in establishing the modalities of rhetoric. Ruth Ann Clark and Jesse G. Delia address this issue in "*Topoi* and Rhetorical Competence" when they indicate that "in any interaction situation participants must generate some shared conception of the norms governing conduct if interaction is to proceed smoothly" (192).

The importance of heuristic procedures for discovering appropriate starting points are also important in discovering the most sensitive mode of expression in group writing. One of the most convincing statements of how a heuristic process such as the enthymeme is bound to the listeners' presumptions is Lloyd Bitzer's "Aristotle's Enthymeme Revisited" in which he claims that enthymemes occur "only when speaker and audience jointly produce them" and that "owing to the skill of the speaker, the audience itself helps construct the proofs by which it is persuaded" (151).

In addition to facilitating the synthesis of starting points for discussion in speaking situations, classical rhetoric can also provide heuristics for establishing the modalities of collaborative expression in writing. All of us have experienced that there are appropriate modes of expression at faculty meetings and other appropriate modes of expression at poker games. Both are group situations and each requires sensitivity to what modes of address are appropriate. Yet what is operating in these two apparently distinct groups is essentially similar: a sensitivity to the conventional modalities of expression as well as the appropriate *topoi* that captures the inferential patterns shared between rhetors and auditors. In academic groups or meetings, there is a presumption that a formalized style of expression and mode of reasoning is both appropriate and necessary. In writing groups, the effectiveness of the discourse is in part determined by the degree of congruence of thought and expression between individuals, both within the group and among its readers. In less formal situations, as in the poker game, informal styles in group discussion are also presumed; that is, under certain conditions no one in a group expects elaborate, apodectic structures of causal reasoning for warranting claims and would probably find such structuring to be contrived, tedious, and inappropriate.

Writing group members are frequently encouraged to express points in a spontaneous manner, which usually exhibits itself in a cumulative, loosely constructed style in which one idea is progressively added to the next. Yet while spontaneity is beneficial, so is the need for structuring the environment and framework within which it occurs. Two points critical to applying the heuristics of classical rhetoric to group writing now should be underscored. First, there is the importance of determining what the group expects (and accepts) as both personal fact and public knowledge (Bitzer, "Rhetoric and Public Knowledge") and of the ranking of personal preferences into an agreed-upon hierarchy of values used as the starting points upon which collaborative ideas are expressed. Second is the importance of realizing the appropriate modalities of expression for the group. Classical rhetoric provides heuristics to deal with both of these concerns.

Classical Rhetoric and Collaborative Argument

The heuristic processes for structuring and evaluating rhetorical discourse in group writing discussed here are grounded in classical rhetoric and are particularly appropriate for argumentative composition. An analogy highlights the utility of such heuristics. When students go to law or business schools, they usually learn by the case method. A seemingly endless number of cases are presented and argued and, out of this process, the "smart" students not only learn more than the obvious heuristic tricks of argument but also learn how to think as a lawyer or an executive. The best professional schools claim to teach this ability but often do it, as Maurice Natenson claims, indirectly; that is, such programs change how people generate ideas, make inferences, and express thoughts. In short, they place them in the manner and mode in which professionals in the field should think and communicate. Similarly, heuristic procedures growing out of classical rhetoric have established clearly structured systems of thought and expression that can be applied explicitly to group writing. The following example of a system using principles of classical rhetoric illustrates such heuristic processes.

In classical rhetoric an argument is called for because there is a problematic situation that has incompatible alternatives whose merits are in dispute. Classical heuristics aid in focusing on the central point (or *stasis*) and in establishing the starting points that must be first agreed on for resolution to occur. After such agreement is reached, criteria ranking argumentative modalities, goals, and values are explicitly articulated and established in an agreed-upon hierarchy (Young et al. 92–96). This hierarchy of values and agreed-upon modalities of argument are the basis upon which positions are advanced for deliberation. After agreement at this level of argument is attained, potential solutions are advanced to enact and thereby realize the position, and these solutions also are subjected to continued deliberation. Clearly, in such a process of composition, a writing group must reach some sort of consensus or (at minimum) acquiescence before composition; they seek, in effect, to become of one mind, the mind of a single rhetor before that view is expressed to readers. Out of this prewriting process a position is formed based on the previously established presumptions. The classical rhetorical implications for the use of this system in group argument are central because each phase of the procedure is based upon an explicit synthesis of agreement by members of the writing group in the form of shared agreement about heuristic processes and argumentative modalities.

The modification of heuristic processes from a single rhetor to group writers requires individuals to adapt to a particular group. This ad hoc adaptation requires that each member's individualized system and argumentative modalities be directed to validity as collectively agreed upon by the group. In brief, arguments are valid only as judged by others, and as all argumentative discourse in group situations is obviously directed toward others, first within the group and then to auditors, such arguments must be *ad hominem*. That is, as Henry W. Johnstone, Jr., claims, *ad hominem* arguments involve "the criticism of a position in terms of its own presuppositions" (*Validity and Rhetoric*).

Group-written argument requires a synthesis of group rationality. Consequently, all argument must be directed toward a collective notion of acceptance and validity within the group, or agreement cannot be attained. If there is no shared basis of agreement for the heuristic presumptions and argumentative modalities, there can be no collective sense of validity for arguments and no shared basis for their evaluation. Operating at the essence of group-written argument is a grounding of what constitutes the reality of the group, that is, the hierarchy of values and argumentative modalities that are the basis for group argument. Having a thorough understanding of these heuristic processes not only helps to understand the argument that is generated but also how and why misunderstanding occurs in these situations.

We need in such situations to move from multiautonomous sets of personal rhetorics to a group rhetoric by displaying and articulating such heuristic procedures as mentioned earlier. Individual discourse may be argumentative (or logical) but not reasonable in that it ignores — or is insensitive to — a synthetic argument in group situations. Part of the function of group writing is to seek a synthesis of these multirhetorical perspectives in an effort to arrive at a collective set of presumptions of what constitutes proof of claims and appropriate modalities of arguments. Thus one of the goals of group writing is that a synthesis of response to a rhetorical situation is preceded by a synthesis of these multirhetorical perspectives, a condition that classical rhetoric can facilitate.

Failure to acknowledge these perspectives can lead to ineffective group interaction and, resultingly, counterproductivity in the writing process. Without providing heuristic presuppositions, arguments can more easily be waived away, ignored, replaced by arbitrary choice, agreed to for the wrong reasons, or even left to force. With a synthesis of heuristic presuppositions, however, group members can more clearly track out argument — see explicitly the values driving another person's perspective — and subsequently use such heuristic processes to adjudicate the merits of the point at issue, systematically directing themselves toward a resolution of the problem. The group that uses the heuristics of classical rhetoric establishes an environment to encourage synthesis rather than advocacy. Without this collective notion, the group is reduced to a gathering of autonomous writers, each declaiming his or her thesis. How effectively a group orchestrates procedures for resolving problems influences not only the efficiency of consensus but also its quality since the implementation of heuristics can provide sensitive procedures toward generating resolutions. The group effort at problem solving thus requires an artificial creation of heuristic systems.

Summary

Several points made throughout this essay can now be brought into focus. First, it is apparent that rhetoric is inherent in the process of group writing. Collaborators must, if they are to be collaborators, work together to form a shared view on not only the nature of the problem that brings them into the writing situation but also the techniques of reasoning and patterns of presentation to be used in advancing a solution. Thus for the prewriting phase of the process to be effective, contributors must seek to attain agreement of both objective and route. To do so heuristic processes of conceptualization and articulation of individual opinions must be synthesized. Classical heuristics provide systems for establishing hierarchies of values and argumentative modalities as a precondition for arriving at the point at issue and advancing positions and thus, in group writing situations, provide an opportunity to articulate individual views. Second, this modified classical system constantly encourages synthesis rather than autonomous advocacy by building in opportunities for discussion and interchange at significant junctions leading to group consensus. Such is the case with presumptions grounding argumentative modes, defining the problematic situation and point at issue, and structuring the hierarchy of values leading to the formulation of a position and consensus. Third, Johnstone argues in "From Philosophy to Rhetoric and Back" that rhetoric need not be unilateral, directive, and manipulative but can be bilateral by a mutual exposing of techniques.

In their recently published book, *Singular Texts/Plural Authors: Perspectives on Collaborative Writing,* Andrea Lunsford and Lisa Ede offer a summary of the characteristics of successful collaborative writing assignments (123–24). Included among these characteristics are the opportunity for group cohesion, the invitation for collaboration, the possibility for the evolution of group norms and the negotiation of both authority and responsibility, the encouragement of creative conflict and protection of minority views, and the allowance for peer and self-evaluation of assignment and performance. It should be clear that the adaptation of the heuristics of classical rhetoric can do much to assist in the realization of these characteristics. In respect to the specific topic under discussion, rhetoric in the process of group writing need not be unilateral but may be multilateral if a synthesis of heuristic processes and argumentative modalities is attained.

At every significant juncture in the writing process there is the opportunity for a synthesis of argumentative perspectives. In this respect, writers who comprise the group not only form agreement on task and techniques; they also have the potential of forming one collective mind directed toward a synthesis of rationality through a unification of the processes mentioned above. Recognition of these points will make apparent the importance of establishing explicit heuristic processes for group writing tasks that facilitate a synthesis of argumentative perspectives with clearly recognizable points of agreement. The importance of such a system was recognized by classical rhetoricians for individual, public discourse, and such procedures for argument are a system that can be easily modified to enhance the conditions necessary for productive collaboration in group-writing situations. There are few tasks more exciting for theoreticians of classical rhetoric than to reexamine heuristic processes as a generating force for thinking rhetorically, for it means that individuals benefit from the systems of classical rhetoric and their potential to generate new ways of knowing.

While the study of classical rhetoric is often done for historical accuracy and enrichment, work by scholars such as Edward P.J. Corbett and Winifred Bryan Horner, who have devoted much of their scholarly career to demonstrating its application to contemporary rhetoric and composition, have made its use and benefit to current writing apparent. To study classical rhetoric for its own historical worth has long been established as a laudable scholarly pursuit ("The Classical Tradition(s) of Rhetoric"). To study classical rhetoric for a more sensitive understanding of contemporary writing is not only a pursuit of equal merit but one that reaffirms the original task of classical rhetoric before it was "classical" and was known only as rhetoric.

Note

1. A substantially revised version of an article appearing in *Small Group Behavior* (May 1985), this essay is fittingly dedicated to Winifred

Bryan Horner, whose career is devoted not only to enriching our knowledge of rhetoric's history but to applying that knowledge to contemporary concerns in rhetoric and composition.

Works Cited

Bitzer, Lloyd F. "Aristotle's Enthymeme Revisited." *Quarterly Journal of Speech* 45 (1959): 399–408. Rpt. *Aristotle: The Classical Heritage of Rhetoric*. Ed. Keith V. Erickson. Metuchen, NJ: Scarecrow, 1974. 141–55.

————. "Rhetoric and Public Knowledge." *Rhetoric, Philosophy, and Literature: An Exploration*. Ed. Don M. Burks. West Lafayette, IN: Purdue UP, 1978. 67–93.

Chomsky, Noam. "A Review of B. F. Skinner's Verbal Behavior." *The Structure of Language: Readings in the Philosophy of Language*. Ed. Jerry A. Fodor and Jerrold J. Katz. Englewood Cliffs, NJ: Prentice-Hall, 1964. 547–78.

Clark, Ruth Ann, and Jesse G. Delia. "*Topoi* and Rhetorical Competence." *Quarterly Journal of Speech* 65 (1979): 187–206.

Corbett, Edward P.J. *Classical Rhetoric and the Modern Student*. 3rd ed. New York: Oxford UP, 1990.

————. "The Usefulness of Classical Rhetoric." *College Composition and Communication* 14 (1963): 162–64. Rpt. in *Selected Essays of Edward P.J. Corbett*. Ed. Robert J. Connors. SM Studies in Composition and Rhetoric. Dallas, TX: Southern Methodist UP, 1989. 14–21.

D'Angelo, Frank. *A Conceptual Theory of Rhetoric*. Cambridge, MA: Winthrop, 1975.

Enos, Richard Leo. "Classical Rhetoric and Group Decision Making: A Relationship Warranting Further Inquiry." *Small Group Behavior* 16 (1985): 235–44.

————. "The Classical Tradition(s) of Rhetoric: A Demur to the Country Club Set." *College Composition and Communication* 38 (1987): 283–90.

Enos, Richard Leo, and Janice M. Lauer. "The Meaning of *Heuristic* in Aristotle's *Rhetoric* and Its Implications for Contemporary Rhetorical Theory." *A Rhetoric of Doing: Essays on Written Discourse in Honor of James L. Kinneavy*. Ed. Stephen P. Witte, Neil Nakadate, and Roger D. Cherry. Carbondale: Southern Illinois UP, 1992. 79–87.

Gere, Anne Ruggles. *Writing Groups: History, Theory, and Implications*. Published for the Conference on College Composition and Communication: Studies in Writing & Rhetoric. Carbondale: Southern Illinois UP, 1987.

Grimaldi, William M. A., S. J. "The Auditors' Role in Aristotelian Rhetoric." *Oral and Written Communication: Historical Approaches.* Ed. Richard Leo Enos. Newbury Park, CA: Sage, 1990. 65–81.

Horner, Winifred Bryan. *Rhetoric in the Classical Tradition.* New York: St. Martin's, 1988.

Janda, Mary Ann. "Collaboration in a Traditional Classroom Environment." *Written Communication* 7 (1990): 291–315.

Johnstone, Henry. W., Jr. "From Philosophy to Rhetoric and Back." *Rhetoric, Philosophy, and Literature: An Exploration.* Ed. Don M. Burks. West Lafayette, IN: Purdue UP, 1978. 49–66.

———. *Validity and Rhetoric in Philosophical Argument: An Outlook in Transition.* University Park, PA: Dialogue Press of Man & World, 1978.

LeFevre, Karen Burke. *Invention as a Social Act.* Published for the Conference on College Composition and Communication: Studies in Writing & Rhetoric. Carbondale: Southern Illinois UP, 1987.

Lunsford, Andrea, and Lisa Ede. *Singular Texts/Plural Authors: Perspectives on Collaborative Writing.* Carbondale: Southern Illinois UP, 1990.

Natenson, Maurice. "The Arts of Indirection." *Rhetoric, Philosophy, and Literature: An Exploration.* Ed. Don M. Burks. West Lafayette, IN: Purdue UP, 1978. 35–47.

Perelman, Chaim, and L. Olbrechts-Tyteca. *The New Rhetoric: A Treatise on Argumentation.* Trans. John Wilkinson and Purcell Weaver. Notre Dame, IN: U of Notre Dame P, 1969.

Welch, Kathleen E. *The Contemporary Reception of Classical Rhetoric: Appropriations of Ancient Discourse.* Hillsdale, NJ: Lawrence Erlbaum, 1990.

Young, Richard E., Alton Becker, and Kenneth L. Pike. *Rhetoric: Discovery and Change.* New York: Harcourt, 1970.

11 Conversation Versus Declamation as Models of Written Discourse

S. Michael Halloran

Over the past several years, a body of literature has developed suggesting an extended analogy between written discourse and conversation. In a 1980 article in *College English,* for example, Charles Bazerman postulates a "conversational model" as a means of articulating the relationship between reading and writing. Kenneth Bruffee's work on collaborative learning invokes philosopher Michael Okeshott's notion of "the conversation of mankind" as a model for what might go on in the writing classroom. Karen Burke LeFevre's monograph, *Invention as a Social Act,* invokes Kenneth Burke's image of intellectual life as an endless party conversation as the basis for an analysis of rhetorical invention. Deborah Tannen and other discourse analysts find strong connections between writing and various forms of spoken discourse, including conversation. Gregory Clark's *Dialogue, Dialectic, and Conversation: A Social Perspective on the Function of Writing* develops an extended theory with pedagogical implications based on the analogy between writing and conversation. And the widespread interest in such concepts as "dialogics" and "discourse communities" strongly implies, if it does not explicitly employ, a conversational model for understanding written discourse.

What these various conversational models all suggest is that we should view writing not as the making of an artifact, but as response to what others have said and written and as invitation to further response by others. A text becomes analogous to a "turn" in conversation. A simple question this growing and provocative literature tends to slight is, Conversation as opposed to what? The question is important for at least two reasons. First,

156

to understand what anything is, we have to have a reasonably clear sense of what it is not. Second, in the absence of a clear alternative, "the conversational model" can degenerate into a slogan. The implication one takes from at least some of the literature on a conversational model is that teaching in a nonconversational mode is self-evidently deficient. Conversational teaching and writing—which also goes under such headings as collaborative, or social, or dialogical—is valorized as The Right Way, and the unexplicated alternative becomes by implication The Wrong Way, something like the Victorian spectre of onanism—a degrading practice that may make you crazy.

In this essay I hope to do two things. First, I will try to articulate more fully the monological model that proponents of conversational models are trying to supplant and provide some historical perspective on both conversational and monological models. Then I will propose that a conversational model should be understood not as replacement for something outmoded, but as a kind of dialectical complement to its alternative, which I will call the "declamatory" model. The declamatory model, I will argue, has dominated the teaching of composition since the nineteenth century and perhaps before, and because of the fundamental nature of the composition course will continue to exercise a powerful influence. The emerging conversational model acts as corrective to the declamatory model, but a purely conversational view of writing would be as narrow and deficient as a purely declamatory one.

But first, let me explain what I mean by a "model." Both the practice and the teaching of discourse I take to be arts in something like Aristotle's sense of that term. We speak, write, and teach quite naturally and inevitably, and it is clear from our experience that some people do one or more of these things more effectively than other people do. This being the case, it ought to be possible to tease out of the practices of those who speak, write, and teach well some principles for improving both the practice and the teaching of discourse. The body of those principles would constitute an art.[1] I understand a model as simply an elaborated metaphor that serves to organize and focus some of the principles of an art. As with a scientific model, there is nothing inevitable about a given model for discourse; it is simply more or less useful toward certain ends.

My point here is that as the scientist can usefully entertain the apparently contradictory notion that light is both particle and wave, so too the rhetorician might usefully conceive discourse as both conversation and something quite unlike conversation. Aristotle proposed "dialectic," something I take to be similar to conversation, as his model for rhetoric. The author of the *Rhetorica ad Herrenium* took "making a speech," something I take to be similar to declamation, as his model. We need not reject one in choosing the other because the activity of making and sharing meaning in language is more complex than either model can reveal. The usefulness of a model lies precisely in its ability to bring certain features into clear focus by filtering out other features. Or, as Kenneth Burke would say, the model may produce a "trained incapacity." In learning to see a thing in one way, I learn not to see it in other ways that might have their own validity and value. The corrective is to use alternative models that complement each other and to bear in mind that a model is just that—a model—and not a definitive depiction of the thing modeled.

The model I am proposing as a dialectical alternative to conversation is declamation. I am thinking of the practice of speaking for display that flourished throughout the classical period, especially during the period called the Second Sophistic at Rome. Declamation was practiced by both accomplished orators and students from the time of the original Greek sophists and would remain an important school exercise up through the eighteenth and into the nineteenth centuries. And, as I will try to show shortly, the writing done in composition classes of our own time can be understood as a form of declamation.

The surviving speeches of Gorgias ("Defense in Behalf of Palamedes" and "Encomium of Helen") appear to be declamations whose purpose was simply to demonstrate the great artistry of the orator and thus advertise his services as a teacher. What marks them as declamations is not their form but their detachment from any immediate rhetorical problem. Palamedes was not in fact on trial, and there was, so far as we know, no actual ceremonial occasion calling for a speech in praise of Helen. They adopt the forms of what we might call, for want of a better term, "real" rhetorical discourse—the Helen of epideictic speech, the Palamedes of forensic—but the ceremonial and judicial forums are imaginary. Both speeches are utterly disinterested so far as the public life of the time is concerned. In this sense they are pure aesthetic objects, though they also bear some similarity to modern-day advertising.

The practice of declamation eventually became a standard rhetorical exercise for students who had moved beyond the graded forms of the *progymnasmata*. Among the set themes for declamation recorded by Seneca, for example, are Agamemnon deliberating with himself whether to sacrifice Iphigenia, and Cicero similarly deliberating whether to beg forgiveness of Anthony. There were also intricate forensic cases, based on wild coincidence or convoluted relationships. As Gorgias had done in his speeches, the students were expected to imagine a rhetorical exigence and adopt the forms of deliberative or forensic speech. But the discourse was in fact unconnected to life, public or private. The speech was response to nothing more than a set task, and it invited no response from its audience other than the teacher's criticism. With the demise of the Roman republic and the consequent atrophy of any real deliberative function for rhetoric, declamation became an increasingly important activity for accomplished orators as well as for students. Stripped of much of its function in what Yeats would one day call "this pragmatic pig of a world," rhetoric became a fine art through the practice of declamation.

The modern composition classroom necessarily creates a motive to write that is closely analogous to that of the sophistical declaimer. Within the framework of the course, the student is by definition a *writer;* his or her function is to produce papers, and much of our pedagogical literature focuses on how to conjure up audiences and purposes for those papers. Similarly, the sophist was by definition an orator; his job was to make speeches, even when there was no actual rhetorical problem calling for a speech. Set themes about mythological or historical characters provided him with an occasion for doing his job, which was to "make a speech."

This point will perhaps be clearer if we think of it in terms of Lloyd Bitzer's concept of a rhetorical situation. According to Bitzer, a rhetorical situation begins with an exigence, "a need characterized by urgency" and capable of being modified by discourse addressed to a specific audience. A student, for example, faces a choice between two courses and brings the question to her faculty adviser. The student's dilemma over which course to elect constitutes the exigence, and the professor stands in a position to modify the exigence — to help the student resolve her dilemma — through advisory or deliberative discourse. According to this model, rhetorical discourse is always instrumental; it is a means toward the end of modifying the exigence. In the situation of the sophistical declaimer or the student in a composition course, this means-end relationship is inverted; discourse is itself the end, and an "exigence" is fabricated as means toward the end of enabling the student to produce discourse.

In my role as composition teacher, for example, I might pose for my students something like the dilemma sketched above: "A friend has asked for your advice on whether to elect Introduction to Philosophy or Elementary Economics; write a three-page letter advising her on how to decide." But in this case the supposed exigence — the student's dilemma — is means rather than end. I have imagined it in order to enable the real students in my class to fulfill their real end, which is to produce a paper. Similarly, the sophistical declaimer imagined an exigence — Agamemnon's dilemma, for example — as a means toward his end of making a speech.

Rhetorical discourse as Bitzer conceives it conforms reasonably well to the conversational model. The exigence that in his terms "invites discourse" is like a question posed, and the discourse itself a response. When that hypothetical student brings her dilemma over course selection to me as her adviser, what ensues will be quite literally a conversation that will end, or at least pause for a while, with her decision on a course and my signing the inevitable form. But a few weeks hence she may be back in my office with a new dilemma opening up a new conversation or perhaps a new episode in the same conversation. And our ongoing conversation about her choices in the curriculum may eventually develop into a larger and longer conversation about the nature of education, of knowledge, of discipline and life itself, a conversation that may extend well beyond the four years of the undergraduate curriculum and the four walls of my office.

We are moving here, I think you must realize, in the general direction of Okeshott's "conversation of mankind," with Thomas Jefferson responding to Locke, and Martin Luther King, Jr. responding to Thoreau and Ghandi and Jesus. Texts like Lee Jacobus's *A World of Ideas* and Bazerman's *The Informed Writer* attempt to use conversation in this grand sense as a model for a course in composition. An approach such as Bruffee's attempts to use conversation in a more immediate sense by making of the class itself a community that "converses" through writing addressed to classmates. An approach that combines both the grand and the more local and immediate senses of conversation is that of John Gage, based on the articulation of "structural enthymemes" deriving from discussions of readings and issues. But whatever the scale of the "conversation," the means-end relationship posited by Bitzer's concept of rhetorical situation is inverted: while it may achieve authenticity, a classroom "conversation" begins as an artifact of the pedagogy. The one thing everyone knows at the outset of any composition course is that the students will write papers and the teacher will evaluate them. The "conversations" set up by pedagogical theory are thus imaginary in origin, like the trial of Palamedes or the dilemma of Agamemnon.

If I am correct in placing John Gage with the proponents of a conversational model, then the conversational perspective has explicit historical roots that go back very nearly as far as those of the declamatory alternative, an important point missed in Bruffee's discussions of collaboration and conversation. Gage bases his pedagogy on a reading of Aristotle's *Rhetoric,* particularly of the sections dealing with the enthymeme, a reading he derives in part from the interpretation of William Grimaldi. According to this view, the enthymeme or rhetorical syllogism works because it rests on an implied premise assumed to be true by both speaker and audience. The art of rhetoric, then, includes being able to figure out what can "go without saying" before a particular audience. As in the art of conversation, it is equally important to know both what to say and what not to say. I will come back to this emphasis the conversational model gives to what may be left unsaid, but for now I want only to make the point that the conversational model should not be seen as a recent innovation. In addition to the Aristotelian concept of enthymeme, it can be connected with the classical theory of stasis, which emphasized analysis of the question at issue in a controversy, and to the practice of disputation, which engaged students in a formal process of verbal exchange that can be seen as a highly ritualized conversation. Like its monological alternative, the conversational model can be seen as a powerful tendency that waxes and wanes, but never entirely disappears, throughout the tradition of rhetorical studies.

One might, in fact, look at the history of rhetoric as a continuing dialectic between conversational and declamatory tendencies. Ong's view of Ramism as a "decay of dialogue" could be recast as an ascendency of the declamatory tendency over the conversational. The evolution in this country from the Ramistic rhetoric of the seventeenth and early eighteenth centuries to the neo-Ciceronianism of the mideighteenth through early nineteenth centuries could then be seen as the reemergence of the conversational tendency. And the supplanting of neo-Ciceronianism by current-traditional rhetoric would be the declamatory tendency once again asserting itself.

Such an account of rhetorical history may or may not be worth pursuing. But from the pedagogical and theoretical viewpoints, I would argue that we need both conversational and declamatory models in order to avoid suffering from "trained incapacity."

In a 1987 *College English* article, Peter Elbow argues for something like the sort of double vision I have in mind, though he frames his case in terms quite different from mine. Elbow sets up an opposition between writing that is consciously addressed to an audience and writing that ignores audience, and then argues that writers often need to forget about audience in order to achieve the full potential of their thoughts and words. He does not urge that audience-directed writing is in any sense "wrong," though he does suggest that we are probably overemphasizing this mode. His position finally is that as theorists and teachers we must be prepared to embrace contraries, to see discourse as both "communication" and "poesis," to teach writing that is both "public" and "private." What Elbow calls "public" writing or discourse as "communication" springs from what I have been calling the conversational model. It is oriented toward some specific rhetorical situation, and thus to a clearly defined audience. What Elbow calls "private" writing or discourse as "poesis" springs from what I have been calling the declamatory model. It is oriented toward no situation at all beyond the blank sheet of paper, and it thus frees the writer to follow the words wherever they choose to go.

Surely Elbow is right in arguing that sometimes—in fact many times—both novice and expert writers need to pursue the logic of their own language without worrying about an audience or a rhetorical exigence. This need becomes clearer still if we consider for a moment the implications of the conversational model's emphasis on "what goes without saying." In learning to participate in professional and civic discourse communities, students must learn what not to say as well as what to say. The importance of this realm of the unsaid is emphasized in rhetorical theory by the concept of the enthymeme, and in the Gricean analysis of conversation by the maxim of quantity: Do not make your contribution more informative than is required. But is it not equally important that sometimes we plunge into the realm of the unspeakable, making explicit and thus available for analysis what ordinarily would remain tacit? Students need to be "acculturated" to the academic discourse community, and for this purpose the conversational model is useful. But they need equally to grow as persons who will live much of their lives beyond the professional world, and who even within that world should be able to challenge the established wisdom that "goes without saying." For this purpose the declamatory model is equally useful. Conversation emphasizes the need to observe established proprieties of discourse, to say what is expected and advance the thinking of a group in a more-or-less predictable direction. Declamation emphasizes the possibility of saying something surprising, of disappointing expectations and striking off in a new direction that may or may not prove fruitful.

The idea that declamation opens up new cultural possibilities suggests another perspective on the surviving speeches of Gorgias, one that can elaborate the social significance of a rhetorical form that on its face seems socially "disengaged." On one level, the speeches of Gorgias are a kind of rhetorical poesis, an exercise of rhetorical artistry outside the context of any "real" rhetorical situation; it is in this sense that they seem disengaged. Yet on another level we might see them as deliberate choices to say what within the established boundaries of the culture was supposed to be unsayable and in that way address questions that had been closed off by established commonplace knowledge. Both Helen and Palamedes were regarded as embodiments of human frailty and error, Helen for having run off with Paris and Palamedes for betraying Achilles. Yet Gorgias undertakes to praise Helen and defend Palamedes, and in so doing he calls into question all the unspoken, rhetorically "unspeakable" assumptions that warranted their placement in Greek demonology.[2] And it is precisely the playful, "unsituated," poetic character of declamation that enables him to do so. Far from being socially irrelevant, a declamation thus may achieve significance more fundamental than the most explicitly situated conversational discourse. In turning away from the exigencies and constraints of an immediate rhetorical situation, in choosing, as Peter Elbow would say, to ignore audience, a rhetor may address issues of far deeper consequence.

But having said this in defense of the declamatory model, I must finally disagree with Elbow's view that the sort of writing that flows from it needs particular emphasis now. As I have already argued, the underlying structure of composition as a course makes the declamatory model an inevitable part of our thinking about rhetoric. In an important sense, composition *is* declamation, and nothing we can do will make it otherwise. Efforts to develop and put into practice a conversational model create a tension with this underlying declamatory structure, a tension that is healthy for two reasons. It will direct our and our students' attention to the very different (read "conversational") structure of rhetorical situations outside the academic world—in the world we too often, yet understandably, characterize as "the real world," as if the one in the classroom were more fictitious than that other.

The more important reason we should strive to make the inherently declamatory writing of the classroom more conversational is this: doing so can help us to see and exploit the socially disruptive potential of declamation. What is finally essential is the tension of our efforts to use both models, to see writing as both declamation and conversation. In the world of business or politics, where discourse is governed by the conventions of a well-defined community, the harder term of the equation to keep alive will be declamation. But in the composition classroom, where writing papers is one's reason for being there and audiences must be found, the conversational side will be more difficult to sustain and hence the one most in need of theoretical development.

Notes

1. Here I am deliberately paraphrasing the passage in book I, chapter 1, of the *Rhetoric* in which Aristotle sketches his rationale for rhetoric being an art.

2. I am indebted to Kathryn Conway for pointing out that the "Encomium of Helen" can be read as the literal defense of a woman, and in this sense as an attack on the cultural assumptions that made her an icon of guilt.

Works Cited

Ad C. Herennium (Rhetorica ad Herennium). Trans. Harry Caplan. Cambridge: Harvard UP, 1968.

Aristotle. *The Rhetoric and the Poetics of Aristotle*. Trans. W. Rhys Roberts and Ingram Bywater. New York: Modern Library, 1954.

Bazerman, Charles. *The Informed Writer: Using Sources in the Disciplines*. Boston: Houghton, 1989.

———. "A Relationship Between Reading and Writing: The Conversational Model." *College English* 41 (1980): 656–61.

Bitzer, Lloyd. "The Rhetorical Situation." *Philosophy and Rhetoric* 1 (1968): 1–14.

Bruffee, Kenneth A. "Collaborative Learning and 'The Conversation of Mankind.'" *College English* 46 (1984): 635–52.

———. "Social Construction, Language, and the Authority of Knowledge: a Bibliographical Essay." *College English* 48 (1986): 773–90.

Clark, Gregory. *Dialogue, Dialectic, and Conversation: A Social Perspective on the Function of Writing.* Carbondale: Southern Illinois UP, 1990.

Elbow, Peter. "Closing My Eyes as I Speak: An Argument for Ignoring Audience." *College English* 49 (1987): 50–69.

Gage, John T. "An Adequate Epistemology for Composition: Classical and Modern Perspectives." *Essays on Classical Rhetoric and Modern Discourse.* Ed. Robert J. Connors, Lisa S. Ede, and Andrea A. Lunsford. Carbondale: Southern Illinois UP, 1984.

———. *The Shape of Reason: Argumentative Writing in College.* New York: Macmillan, 1987.

Gage, John T., and Erling Nielsen. "Assignment and Commentary." *What Makes Writing Good: A Multiperspective.* Ed. William E. Coles, Jr. and James Vopat. Lexington, MA: D. C. Heath, 1985. 98–104.

Gorgias. "Encomium of Helen" and "A Defense in Behalf of Palamedes." *The Older Sophists.* Ed. Rosamund Kent Sprague. Trans. George Kennedy. Columbia: U of South Carolina P, 1972. 50–63.

Green, Lawrence D. "Enthymemic Invention and Structural Prediction." *College English* 41 (1980): 623–34.

Grimaldi, William M. A. *Studies in the Philosophy of Aristotle's Rhetoric.* Wiesbaden: Franz Steiner Verlag GMBH, 1972.

Jacobus, Lee A. *A World of Ideas: Essential Readings for College Writers.* Boston: Bedford, 1990.

Kennedy, George. "Declamation," "Seneca the Elder," and "Criticism of Declamation." *The Art of Rhetoric in the Roman World.* Princeton: Princeton UP, 1972. 312–37.

LeFevre, Karen Burke. *Invention as a Social Act.* Carbondale: Southern Illinois UP, 1987.

Ong, Walter J. *Ramus: Method and the Decay of Dialogue.* Cambridge: Harvard UP, 1958.

Sussman, Lewis A. "Early Imperial Declamation: A Translation of the Elder Seneca's Prefaces." *Speech Monographs* 37 (1970): 135–51.

Tannen, Deborah, ed. *Coherence in Spoken and Written Discourse.* Norwood, NJ: Ablex, 1984.

———. *Spoken and Written Language: Exploring Orality and Literacy.* Norwood, NJ: Ablex, 1982.

Winifred Bryan Horner:
A Bibliography

Contributors

Index

Winifred Bryan Horner: A Bibliography

Books and Monographs

Three Nineteenth-Century Scottish Rhetoricians: Aytoun, Bain, and Jardine. Carbondale: Southern Illinois UP, forthcoming.

Nineteenth-Century Scottish Rhetoric: The American Connection. Carbondale: Southern Illinois UP, 1992.

The Present State of Scholarship in Historical and Contemporary Rhetoric. Rev. ed. Columbia: U of Missouri P, 1990.

Hodges Harbrace College Handbook. 11th ed. Coauthored with Suzanne Webb, John C. Hodges, and Mary Whitten, 1990.

Rhetoric in the Classical Tradition. New York: St. Martin's, 1988.

Composition and Literature: Bridging the Gap. Chicago: U of Chicago P, 1983.

Historical Rhetoric: An Annotated Bibliography of Selected Sources in English. Boston: G. K. Hall, 1980.

A Study of Problems in Undergraduate Writing at the University of Missouri. Columbia: U of Missouri, 1970.

Articles and Chapters

"Nineteenth-Century Scottish Rhetoric: The Missing Link." *Festschrift for James Kinneavy.* Ed. Rosalind Gabin. Scholastica, forthcoming.

"Nineteenth-Century Rhetoric at the Universities of Aberdeen and St. Andrews with an Annotated Bibliography of Archival Materials." *Rhetoric Society Quarterly* 20 (Summer 1990): 287–99.

"Nineteenth-Century Rhetoric at the University of Glasgow with an Annotated Bibliography of Archival Materials." *Rhetoric Society Quarterly* 20 (Spring 1990): 173–85.

"The Roots of Writing Instruction: Eighteenth- and Nineteenth-Century Britain." *Rhetoric Review* 7 (1990): 322–45.

"Writing Instruction in Great Britain: Eighteenth and Nineteenth Century." *A Short History of Writing Instruction from Ancient Greece to Twentieth-Century America.* Ed. James J. Murphy. Davis: CA: Hermagoras, 1990. 121–49.

"Nineteenth-Century Rhetoric at the University of Edinburgh with an Annotated Bibliography of Archival Materials." *Rhetoric Society Quarterly* 19 (Fall 1989): 365–75.

"Learning to Write, Writing to Learn." *College Teaching Monographs.* U of North Dakota, 1989.

"Dialectic as Invention: Dialogue in the Writing Center." *Focuses* 1 (Spring 1988): 11–19.

"President's Message." *Journal of Writing Program Administration* (Spring 1985): 5 and (Spring 1986): 5.

"Rhetoric in the Liberal Arts: Nineteenth-Century Scottish Universities." *The Rhetorical Tradition and Modern Writing.* Ed. James J. Murphy. New York: MLA, 1983. 89–95.

"Speech-Act Theory and Writing." *FFORUM: A Newsletter of the English Composition Board, University of Michigan* 3 (Fall 1981): 9–11. Rpt. in *FFORUM: Essays on Theory and Practice in the Teaching of Writing.* Upper Montclair, NJ: Boynton/Cook, 1983. 96–98.

"Freshman Composition: The Long Tradition." *Ball State University Forum* 20 (Autumn 1979): 3–11.

"Speech-Act and Text-Act Theory: 'Theme-ing' in Freshman Composition." *College Composition and Communication* (1979): 165–70.

"The Graduate Student Teacher-Training Program at the University of Missouri." *Options for the Teaching of English.* Ed. Jasper P. Neel. New York: MLA, 1978. 57–62.

Contributors

Edward P.J. Corbett is Professor of English at Ohio State University. He has formerly been director of freshman English at OSU, president of the Ohio Council of Teachers of English Language Arts, chair of the Conference on College Composition and Communication, editor of *College Composition and Communication,* and chair of the College Section of the National Council of Teachers of English. He is the author of *Classical Rhetoric for the Modern Student, The Little English Handbook, Selected Essays of Edward P.J. Corbett* (ed. Robert J. Connors), and *The Writing Teacher's Sourcebook* (with Gary Tate). His many honors include being awarded the Distinguished Scholar Award from Ohio State University and the Distinguished Service Award from NCTE, an honorary membership in the OSU chapter of Phi Beta Kappa, and Rhetorician of the Year at the 1989 Young Rhetoricians' Conference.

Richard Leo Enos received his PhD in 1973 from Indiana University. He is Professor of Rhetoric in the Department of English at Carnegie Mellon University and past president of the Rhetoric Society of America. His research emphasis is in the history of rhetoric with a specialization in classical rhetoric. He has received support for the study of ancient rhetoric from the National Endowment for the Humanities and has done research on Hellenic rhetoric in Greece through the American School of Classical Studies at Athens under the auspices of the Greek Ministry of Science and Culture.

Theresa Enos, founder and editor of *Rhetoric Review,* teaches in the graduate program in rhetoric and composition at the University of Arizona. Besides publishing essays on rhetorical theory in various journals, she is the editor of *A Sourcebook for Basic Writing Teachers* (Random House, 1987) and *Defining the New Rhetorics* (with Stuart C. Brown, Sage Publications, 1992). She currently is editing *The Rhetoric Encyclopedia* (Garland, forthcoming) and writing a book, *Catalyst for Change,* on disciplinary and gender bias in rhetoric and composition programs (Southern Illinois University Press, forthcoming).

171

S. Michael Halloran is Professor of Rhetoric at Rensselaer Polytechnic Institute, where he received the PhD in communication and rhetoric in 1973. His publications include articles on the theory and history of rhetoric, with special emphasis on rhetoric as an art of civic discourse, and on the rhetoric of scientific discourse. He is particularly interested in the history of the rhetorical tradition in America. Professor Halloran has served as director of graduate studies, department chair, and associate dean of humanities and social sciences at Rensselaer, and as president of the Rhetoric Society of America and chair of the Teaching of Writing Division of the Modern Language Association.

Susan C. Jarratt is Associate Professor and Director of College Composition at Miami University in Ohio. Her book *Rereading the Sophists: Classical Rhetoric Refigured* was published in 1991 by Southern Illinois University Press. She has contributed essays to *College English, PRE/TEXT, Rhetoric Review, Philosophy and Rhetoric,* and *Hypatia: A Journal of Feminist Philosophy.* Her current research interests include feminist theory and pedagogy, historiography, and women in the history of rhetoric.

Richard Lloyd-Jones, past NCTE president, past chair of the Conference on College Composition and Communication, was for ten years director of the University of Iowa School of Letters and before that was assistant to John Gerber, department chair, and colleague with Richard Braddock and Carl Klaus in numerous programs relating to training teachers of writing. With Braddock and Lowell Schoer he summarized research on composition; with Elisabeth McPherson and Nancy Prichard he edited the statements supporting the CCCC policy on students' right to their own language; with Klaus and others he designed Primary Trait Scoring; and with Andrea Lunsford he edited the reports of the English Coalition Conference. He received the Distinguished Service Award of the Iowa Council of Teachers of English in 1980, the second Francis Andrew March Award of the Association of Departments of English in 1987, and the first Exemplar Award of the Conference on College Composition and Communication in 1991. He is now in phased retirement at the University of Iowa.

Thomas P. Miller is Assistant Professor of English at the University of Arizona. He teaches undergraduate composition and graduate courses in rhetorical theory and history in the PhD program in rhetoric, composition, and the teaching of English. He also helps supervise the undergraduate writing program. He has published *The Selected Writings of John Witherspoon* (Southern Illinois University Press, 1990) and articles in *College English, Rhetoric Society Quarterly, Journal of Advanced Composition,* and *Rhetoric Review.* He is currently at work on a book on the eighteenth-century origins of college English studies in Ireland, Scotland, America, and the English Dissenting academies. Research for this book has been supported by funding from the National Endowment for the Humanities, Southern Illinois University, and the University of Arizona.

Jean Dietz Moss is director of the graduate rhetoric program in the English Department at the Catholic University of America and the coordinator of rhetoric and composition courses for undergraduates. After completing a BA in philosophy in 1951, she took time out for marriage and children, returning to academe to take a PhD in history from West Virginia University in 1969. Research in Renaissance history led to three articles and the book *Hendrik Niclaes and His Family of Love* (American Philosophical Society, 1981). Her interest in philosophy, history, and the effects of the printed word sparked another program of study and research in the history of rhetoric, begun during her tenure in the English Department at West Virginia University, 1970–81. Experience in teaching composition to freshmen during the reign of the current-traditional paradigm caused her to search for more effective techniques, finding them in concepts and principles of classical rhetoric. Deciding to expand the investigation, she organized a conference at Catholic University in 1983, sponsored by the National Endowment for the Humanities, where scholars knowledgeable about the classical heritage could help college teachers develop materials for the teaching of writing. She edited and published the papers in *Rhetoric and Praxis: The Contribution of Classical Rhetoric to Practical Reasoning* (Catholic University of America Press, 1986). Professor Moss has published twelve essays on Renaissance pedagogy and on the interplay of rhetoric and dialectics by participants in scientific and religious controversies during the Scientific Revolution. Some of these have appeared in *Renaissance Quarterly, Rhetorica,* the *Rhetoric Society Quarterly,* and *Argumentation.* She has a book forthcoming, *The Copernican Question: Rhetoric in the Cause of Science and Religion.*

Donald C. Stewart, who died 13 February 1992, was Professor of English at Kansas State University. The author of *The Authentic Voice; The Versatile Writer; The Eclectic Reader* (with Paul T. Bryant and

Patricia L. Stewart); *My Yellowstone Years;* chapters in *The Rhetorical Tradition and Modern Writing: The Present State of Scholarship in Historical and Contemporary Rhetoric; Classical Rhetoric and Modern Discourse: Papers in Honor of Professor Edward P.J. Corbett; Traditions of Inquiry: Eight Intellectual Portraits;* and numerous articles in *College English, College Composition and Communication, Research in the Teaching of English, Rhetoric Review, English Education,* and the *Journal of Advanced Composition,* he also published freelance work in *The Christian Science Monitor, Parks and Recreation, Fly Fisherman, Montana: The Magazine of Western History, Change, The Journal of the West,* and *Forecast.* In 1983 Professor Stewart was chair of the Conference on College Composition and Communication.

Kathleen E. Welch, Associate Professor of English at the University of Oklahoma, is the author of *The Contemporary Reception of Classical Rhetoric: Appropriations of Ancient Discourse* (1990). She has published articles in *Rhetoric Review, College Composition and Communication, Rhetoric Society Quarterly, The Journal of Advanced Composition, Written Communication,* and other publications. She currently is writing the book *Classical Rhetoric, Literacy, and Electronic Communication.*

Marjorie Curry Woods received her PhD from the Centre for Medieval Studies at the University of Toronto. She has taught at Oberlin College and the University of Rochester and is currently Associate Professor of English at the University of Texas at Austin. Woods's major teaching and research interests are medieval rhetoric and literary criticism and premodern composition pedagogy. She is the author of the essay on the Middle Ages in *A Short History of the Teaching of Writing from Ancient Greece to Twentieth-Century America* (Hermagoras, 1990) and the "Rhetoric" entry in *Medieval England: An Encyclopedia* (forthcoming from Garland Publications), as well as articles in *Acta Conventus Neo-Latini, The Chaucer Review, Allegorica, The Quarterly Journal of Speech,* and *Rhetorica.* Woods edited and translated *An Early Commentary on the* Poetria nova *of Geoffrey of Vinsauf* (New York: Garland, 1985), which received honorable mention for the John Nicholas Brown Award of the Medieval Academy of America, and is working on a book on all of the commentaries on the *Poetria nova.* Woods served as the American secretary-treasurer of the International Association of Neo-Latin Studies from 1983 to 1989. She has been a member of the Governing Council of the International

Society for the History of Rhetoric since 1989, and in 1990 she was elected to the executive committee of the MLA Discussion Group on the History and Theory of Rhetoric and Composition. In 1983 she received an NEH summer stipend and was an NEH senior fellow in 1987–88.

Index